CAMBERWELL & WEST NORWOOD TRAMWAYS

Robert J Harley

Cover picture: Camberwell Green in the early 1950s. (C.Carter)

Cover colours: These are similar to those used on LCC car No 1.

I would like to dedicate this book to the memory of Alan Watkins, friend and fellow tramway enthusiast.

Requiescat in pace.

First published October 1993

ISBN 1 873793 22 7

Design - Deborah Goodridge

Published by Middleton Press
Easebourne Lane
Midhurst
West Sussex
GU29 9AZ
Tel: (0730) 813169

Printed & bound by Biddles Ltd,
Guildford and Kings Lynn

CONTENTS

INTRODUCTION AND ACKNOWLEDGEMENTS

In this second London volume of the Tramway Classics series we remain on the Surrey side of the Thames to take a closer look at the area south of Camberwell Green. Again I am indebted to many for their assistance in assembling the information for this book. Photographs have been supplied by the National Tramway Museum, H.B.Priestley, R.B.Parr, J.H.Meredith, R.J.S.Wiseman, C.Carter, R.Elliott and D.A.Thompson; I thank them for their support of this project. Dave Jones of the LCC Tramways Trust has also helped in finding some elusive views without which the story would have been the poorer. John Wills has again proved a tower of strength in solving a number of problems which arose during the writing of the text. I must also thank J.H.Price for the supplying a number of photographs, for his in-depth knowledge of tramway operation in the area, and for the loan of various maps and documents. The detailed track maps of the late F.Merton Atkins have been a great help and I have consulted official LCC car plans and those drawn by Terry Russell. Last but not least, I acknowledge a huge debt of gratitude to Ted Oakley, the author of the two volume standard work on the LCC tramways.

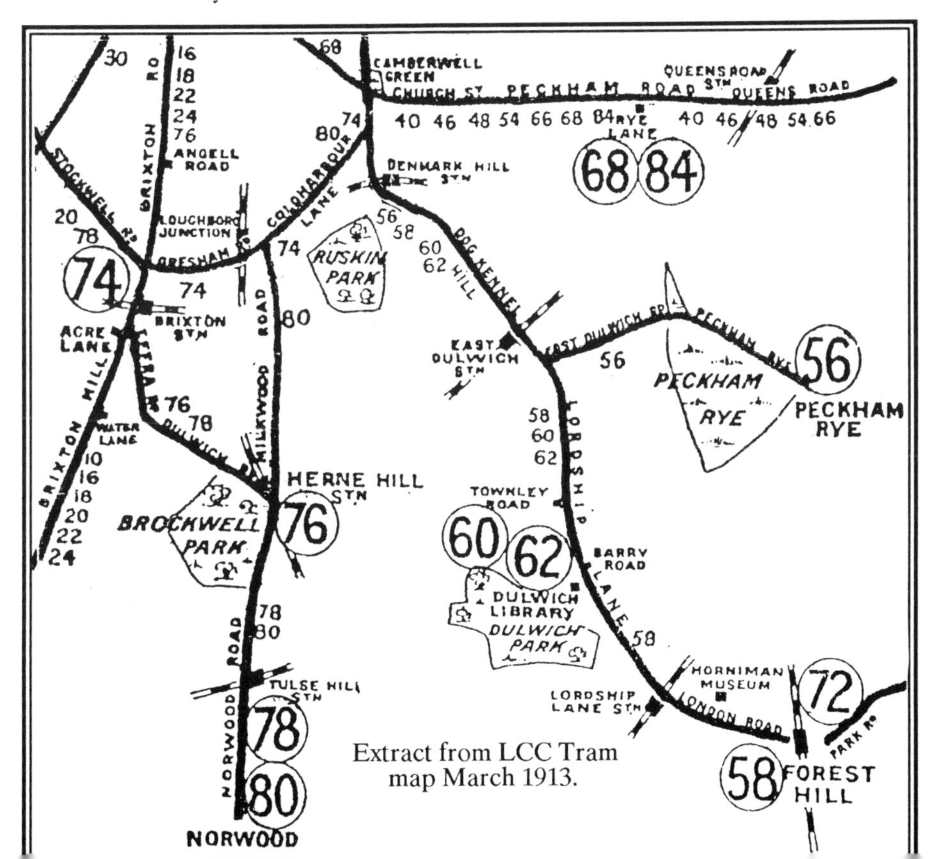

Extract from LCC Tram map March 1913.

GEOGRAPHICAL SETTING

In their time the tramways had to cope with steep gradients and sharp curves, this reflects a landscape of rolling hills and ridges; most of these features have been clothed in an urban mantle for some generations. Greenery is to be found in the open spaces of Peckham Rye, Brockwell Park, Ruskin Park and Dulwich Park. The grounds of the Dulwich estates still present a semi-rural atmosphere in contrast to the surrounding suburbia.

HISTORICAL BACKGROUND

The Camberwell district has been associated in the past with several persons of note, and tradition has it that Queen Boadicea's last stand against the Romans reached a bloody climax on the slopes of Peckham Rye. In less violent times, the composer Mendelssohn once lived in the area and his work "Spring Song" was originally titled Camberwell Green. In the middle of the nineteenth century the main line railway companies started to expand into the district and this created a large house building programme. Horse tramways appeared in 1871 with the opening of the section from the Elephant to Camberwell Green; lines to New Cross opened the next year. A brief hiatus in tramway construction was broken in 1883 when work started on the London Southern Tramways Co. route to West Norwood, Gresham Road and Brixton. In the same year the ill-fated Peckham and East Dulwich Tramways began the task of linking the two areas. The formation of the London County Council led to a new transport policy for the capital which was based on electric tramways using the conduit method of current collection. New electric lines were opened from Camberwell Green to Kennington and Vauxhall in 1903, and to Peckham and New Cross in 1904. The Dulwich hills were tackled in 1906 with a service along Lordship Lane terminating at Barry Road. Peckham Rye was reached with a branch from Goose Green in 1907 and a further extension from Barry Road to Forest Hill was operational at the end of 1908. The tracks on Dog Kennel Hill were quadrupled in 1912 so that the service could be improved and safety maintained on this steep gradient. The cost of new conduit tramways was daunting and the LCC soon tried to persuade local authorities to accept the cheaper overhead wire system. The officers of the council had some success when the wires went up along the reconstructed Coldharbour Lane to Gresham Road section in 1908. Following this, the overhead was used from Loughborough Junction to West Norwood in 1909 and finally from Effra Road to Herne Hill in April 1912. The first change pits in London linking the two forms of electric traction were constructed at Gresham Road, Brixton and at the Camberwell end of Coldharbour Lane. These allowed through cars to operate from the suburban termini to the centre of London. Tramway services then settled down bringing cheap, reliable and pollution-free public transport to every citizen. Improvements in design followed, including faster, more comfortable trams which rode the hills and streets efficiently until the arrival of London Transport in 1933 cast a shadow over tramway operation. The original intention of the new board had been to substitute trolleybuses on the local routes, but the intervention of the Second World War prevented this option. Diesel buses started to take over in 1950 with the replacement of service 34 and choking fumes became the order of the day. This melancholy process came to a conclusion with the last tram passing Camberwell Green in July 1952.

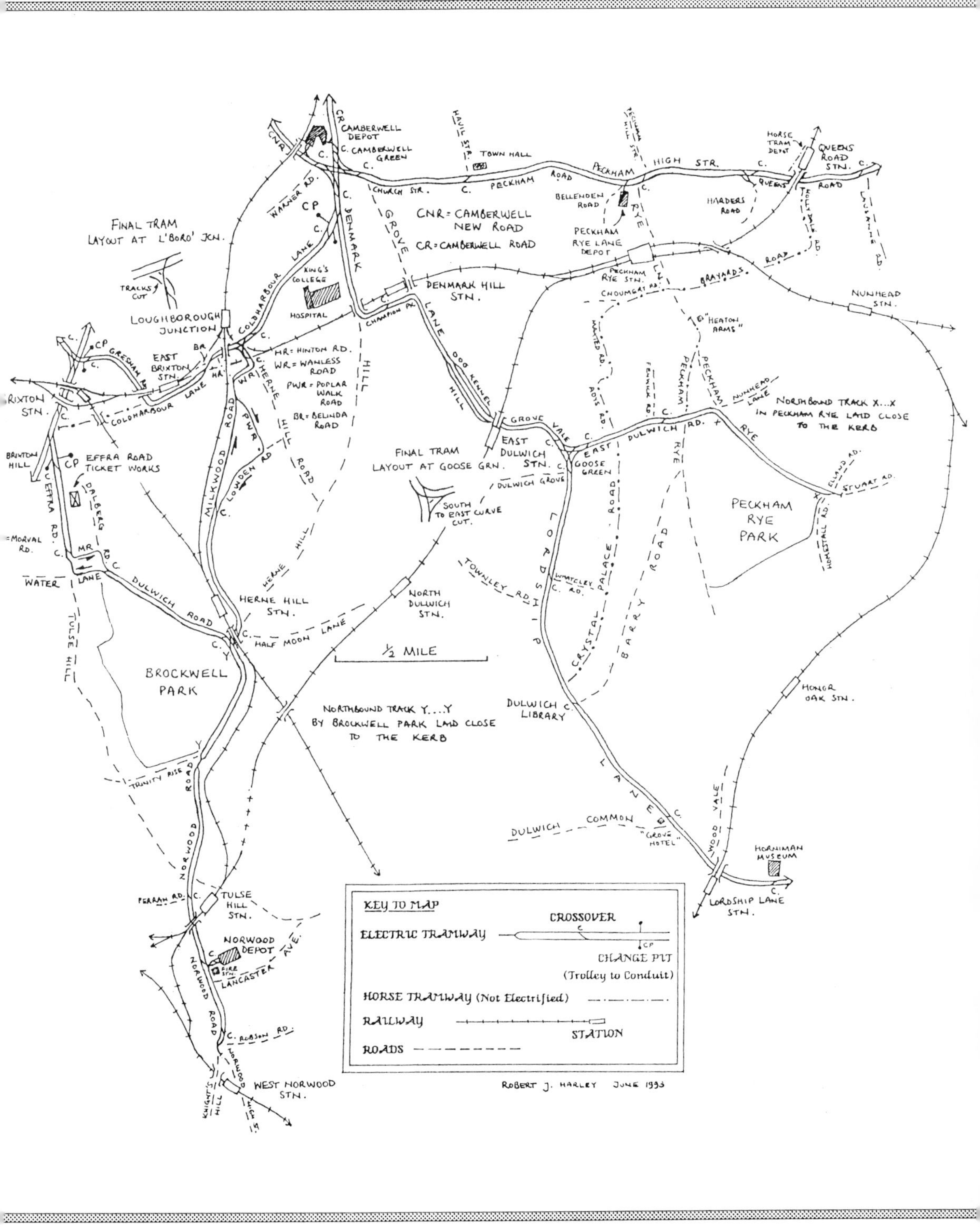

CAMBERWELL DEPOT
C. CAMBERWELL GREEN
CNR
CR
TOWN HALL
PECKHAM HIGH STR.
CHURCH STR.
PECKHAM ROAD
QUEENS ROAD STN.
HORSE TRAM DEPOT
QUEENS ROAD
HARDERS ROAD
BELLENDEN ROAD
PECKHAM RYE LANE DEPOT
PECKHAM RYE STN.
CNR = CAMBERWELL NEW ROAD
CR = CAMBERWELL ROAD
FINAL TRAM LAYOUT AT L'BORO' JCN.
TRACKS CUT
WARNER RD.
DENMARK HILL
GROVE
KING'S COLLEGE HOSPITAL
DENMARK HILL STN.
CHAMPION PK.
CHOUMERT RD.
BRAYARDS
NUNHEAD STN.
"HEATON ARMS"
LOUGHBOROUGH JUNCTION
COLDHARBOUR LANE
EAST BRIXTON STN.
GRESHAM
BRIXTON STN.
HR = HINTON RD.
WR = WANLESS ROAD
PWR = POPLAR WALK ROAD
BR = BELINDA ROAD
DOG KENNEL HILL
GROVE VALE
EAST DULWICH STN.
GOOSE GREEN
EAST DULWICH RD.
PECKHAM RYE
NORTHBOUND TRACK X...X IN PECKHAM RYE LAID CLOSE TO THE KERB
BRIXTON HILL
EFFRA ROAD TICKET WORKS
EFFRA RD.
DALBERG RD.
MORVAL RD.
MR
WATER LANE
HERNE HILL
MILKWOOD ROAD
LOWDEN RD
FINAL TRAM LAYOUT AT GOOSE GRN.
SOUTH TO EAST CURVE CUT.
DULWICH GROVE
LORDSHIP LANE
CRYSTAL PALACE ROAD
BARRY ROAD
PECKHAM RYE PARK
STUART RD.
TOWNLEY RD.
WHATELEY RD.
DULWICH ROAD
HERNE HILL STN.
HALF MOON LANE
NORTH DULWICH STN.
1/2 MILE
TULSE HILL
BROCKWELL PARK
NORTHBOUND TRACK Y...Y BY BROCKWELL PARK LAID CLOSE TO THE KERB
DULWICH LIBRARY
HONOR OAK STN.
TRINITY RISE
NORWOOD ROAD
DULWICH COMMON
"GROVE HOTEL"
WOOD VALE
HORNIMAN MUSEUM
LORDSHIP LANE STN.
FERRAN RD.
TULSE HILL STN.
NORWOOD DEPOT
FIRE STN.
LANCASTER AVE.
ROBSON RD.
KNIGHTS HILL
WEST NORWOOD STN.
KEY TO MAP
ELECTRIC TRAMWAY
CROSSOVER
CHANGE PIT (Trolley to Conduit)
HORSE TRAMWAY (Not Electrified)
RAILWAY
STATION
ROADS
ROBERT J. HARLEY JUNE 1993

1. Camberwell Green to Goose Green

1. A bright spring day long ago, there is time for people to stand and stare outside the *Father Red Cap* public house as a tram in the LCC livery of maroon lake and cream pulls away along Camberwell Road. The tram's status as "king of the road" is yet to be challenged by the internal combustion engine. (J.H.Price Coll.)

2. Rain at Camberwell Green on a dismal Saturday afternoon, 30th September 1950 and the axe is about to fall on service 34. Car 1422 is performing its own march to the scaffold on a last journey from Norwood Depot to Penhall Road scrapyard. (John H.Meredith)

3. The rivals line up. Note the canvas hut for the pointsman rather inconveniently sandwiched between the belisha beacon and the temporary traffic light. On the green light the motorman will guide car 164 over the metalwork in the roadway, hopefully beating the bus to the next stop. (National Tramway Museum. H.B.Priestly)

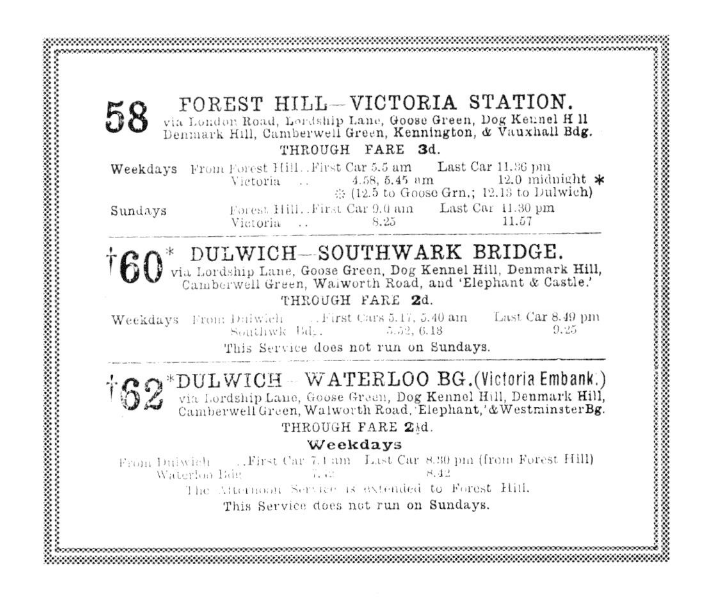

58 FOREST HILL—VICTORIA STATION.
via London Road, Lordship Lane, Goose Green, Dog Kennel Hill
Denmark Hill, Camberwell Green, Kennington, & Vauxhall Bdg.
THROUGH FARE 3d.

Weekdays From Forest Hill . . First Car 5.5 am Last Car 11.36 pm
Victoria . . 4.58, 5.45 am 12.0 midnight *
* (12.5 to Goose Grn.; 12.13 to Dulwich)

Sundays Forest Hill . . First Car 9.0 am Last Car 11.30 pm
Victoria . . 8.25 11.57

†60* DULWICH—SOUTHWARK BRIDGE.
via Lordship Lane, Goose Green, Dog Kennel Hill, Denmark Hill,
Camberwell Green, Walworth Road, and 'Elephant & Castle.'
THROUGH FARE 2d.

Weekdays From Dulwich . . First Cars 5.17, 5.40 am Last Car 8.49 pm
Southwk Bdg. 5.52, 6.18 9.25

This Service does not run on Sundays.

†62*DULWICH—WATERLOO BG. (Victoria Embank.)
via Lordship Lane, Goose Green, Dog Kennel Hill, Denmark Hill,
Camberwell Green, Walworth Road, 'Elephant,' & Westminster Bg.
THROUGH FARE 2½d.

Weekdays

From Dulwich . . First Car 7.1 am Last Car 8.30 pm (from Forest Hill)
Waterloo Bdg 7.42 8.42

The Afternoon Service is extended to Forest Hill.

This Service does not run on Sundays.

Extract from LCC map March 1913.

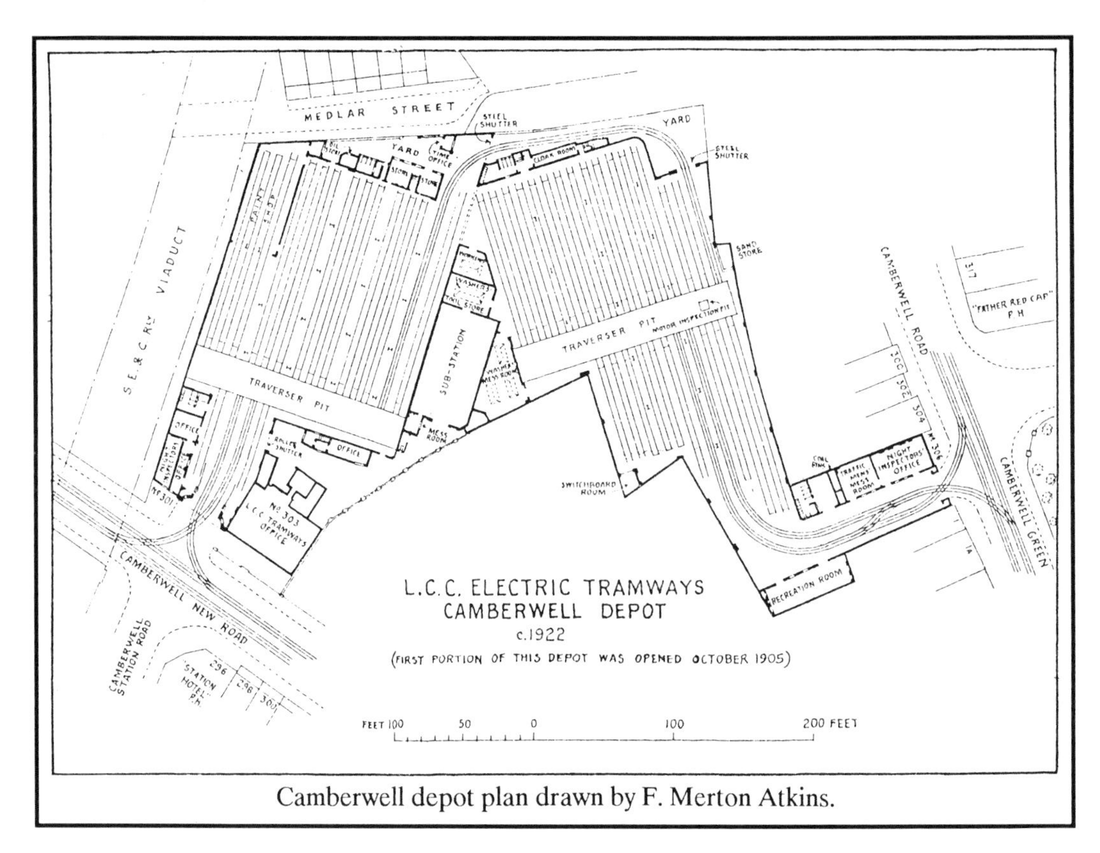

Camberwell depot plan drawn by F. Merton Atkins.

top right

4. LCC cars 408 and 802 cross whilst a four wheel M class car waits to head southwards to Dog Kennel Hill and Goose Green. (R.J.Harley Coll.)

5. At the loading island a crew member peers out from car 1857. Shift changes of tram crews were often made at this location. (R.J.S.Wiseman)

HORSLEYS Ltd
CLAYMORE
WHISKY
DENTIST
40
54
BUCHANAN'S

60
DULWICH LIBRARY
...but Hovis and butter is better
1857
Insist on
VP

6. Tramscape at Camberwell Green. At peak times 250 trams passed across the junction every hour; the local council may have had this in mind when they lobbied, unsuccessfully as it turned out, to have the Bakerloo tube extended from the Elephant and Castle.
(R.J.S.Wiseman)

7. The horse trams of the London Southern Company terminated on a loop just south of the crossroads; here we see a two horse car with transverse "garden" seats on the top deck.
(J.H.Price Coll.)

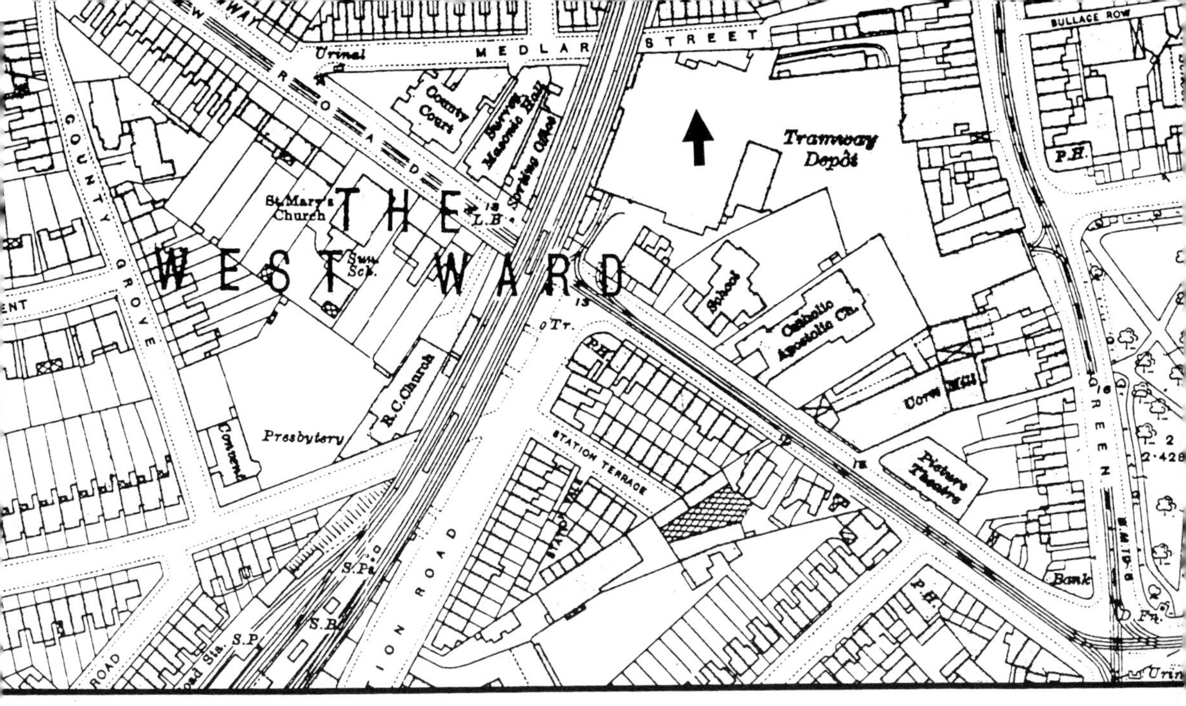

1912 map.

8. The entrance to Camberwell Depot can be seen to the right of car 1922. After the railway bridge Camberwell New Road stretches into the tree lined distance. There was plenty of public transport about in those days! (D.A.Thompson)

58
CAMBERWELL GRN
BISTO

9. Framed by a solid brick arch, an equally robust four motor, eight wheel car on service 58 makes its appearance outside the depot. Camberwell Depot was built on the site of a former horse car shed. In electric days it consisted of two main buildings joined by a connecting spur; the original capacity was 155 trams, but in later years it contained 131 bogie cars. (John H.Meredith)

10. Depots always held a fascination for the enthusiast and in this view taken across the traverser pit, the conduit slots and maintenance pits can clearly be seen. The electric depot was opened in 1905 and the full site was in operation by 1914. It closed to trams in October 1951 and was promptly rebuilt as Walworth bus garage which in turn closed in 1985. However, the story does not end there, because in Melbourne, Australia you can still find a Camberwell Depot full of trams which normally ply the streets of the Victorian Capital. (National Tramway Museum)

11. Appropriately for a tram junction, the *Joiners Arms* plays host to a service 58 car whilst the driver checks the hooded signal box fixed above the traffic light. He will then ease forward confident in the fact that his tram will not veer off right down Coldharbour Lane! (National Tramway Museum. H.B.Priestly)

12. A final view looking towards the Green, shows car 107 which was equipped to work only on conduit lines and did not possess trolley poles. (John H.Meredith)

13. London is justifiably proud of its plane trees, some of which form a natural canopy over car 139 as it traverses the crossover in Champion Park. The tram is flanked on the left side by the railway to Denmark Hill Station and on the right by the imposing William Booth Memorial College. (John H.Meredith)

Send post orders
SURGICAL SERVICE
FREE ADVICE
EXPERT FITTING
SURGICAL SERVICE
SURGICAL SERVICE
DUREX
DUREX
WITH
CARE
YOU'RE
THERE
A.KINSTON
60
CAMBERWELL
107

CARS
STOP
BY REQUEST
84
WALWORTH RD
139

14. A winter's day at the corner of Champion Park with Grove Lane bears witness to the reliability of the tramcar; the service went on through all weathers. The date is 1st January 1951 and it is the last New Year that the tram will see, future winters will see a bus service very prone to disruption in a snowfall. (R.J.S.Wiseman)

16. A fashionable lady of 1951 turns towards the camera as she steps daintily across the tracks trying to avoid getting her heels caught in the rails. This is the start of the four track layout for the gradient of Dog Kennel Hill. Behind car 135 is a nice display of period adverts with "Mr.Therm" pointing the way to a gas powered future. (John H.Meredith)

15. Just past the summit of Dog Kennel Hill a 58 tram halts on its way to Camberwell. It is Christmas Day 1950 and flurries of snow drift across the roadway in this scene from a lost world of long ago. (R.J.S.Wiseman)

17. In this view taken before 1912 a motorman concentrates on the descent, slowing the speed of the car for maximum safety. The reversed stairs next to the driver had holes drilled in them so that he had at least a restricted view of the kerb. In practice this type of stairway was soon replaced by the normal direct type thereby ensuring much better forward vision. (R.J.Harley Coll.)

←

18. The instructions were that no two trams should occupy the same track on the hill in case of brake failure. From the rear of the top deck of a descending car on the inner track, Don Thompson has snapped the following tram coming down on the adjacent line. The centre two tracks carried most of the tram traffic at off peak times. (D.A.Thompson)

19. No enthusiasts' tour would have been complete without a halt on the hill. Here we see several bemused LT officials observing the antics of various photographers who are going to some lengths to record the scene for posterity-witness the gentleman with the tripod in the middle of the highway creating his own traffic island for the approaching motor car! (National Tramway Museum)

20. Walking in the road seems to have been quite popular in this early scene before the quadrupling was completed on 23rd April 1912. (R.J.Harley Coll.)

22. On 22nd September 1951 John Meredith was on hand to record car 1868 after it had completed its descent of the 1 in 10 gradient. Could we imagine a similar traffic-free scene nowadays? (John H.Meredith)

21. Although abandonment was not far distant, track renewal continues at the bottom of the hill; to the left of the tram is the Dulwich Hamlet Athletic Ground. (R.J.S.Wiseman)

58
VICTORIA
...and Hovis and butter for tea
1893
84

SOUTHERN ELECTRIC
FREQUENT TRAINS
C·W·S GOODS
CUT
62
1877

23. Passengers board a Victoria bound tram as an 84 emerges from the shadows en route to Peckham Rye. The track repairs continue in the background on this June day in 1951. (R.J.S.Wiseman)

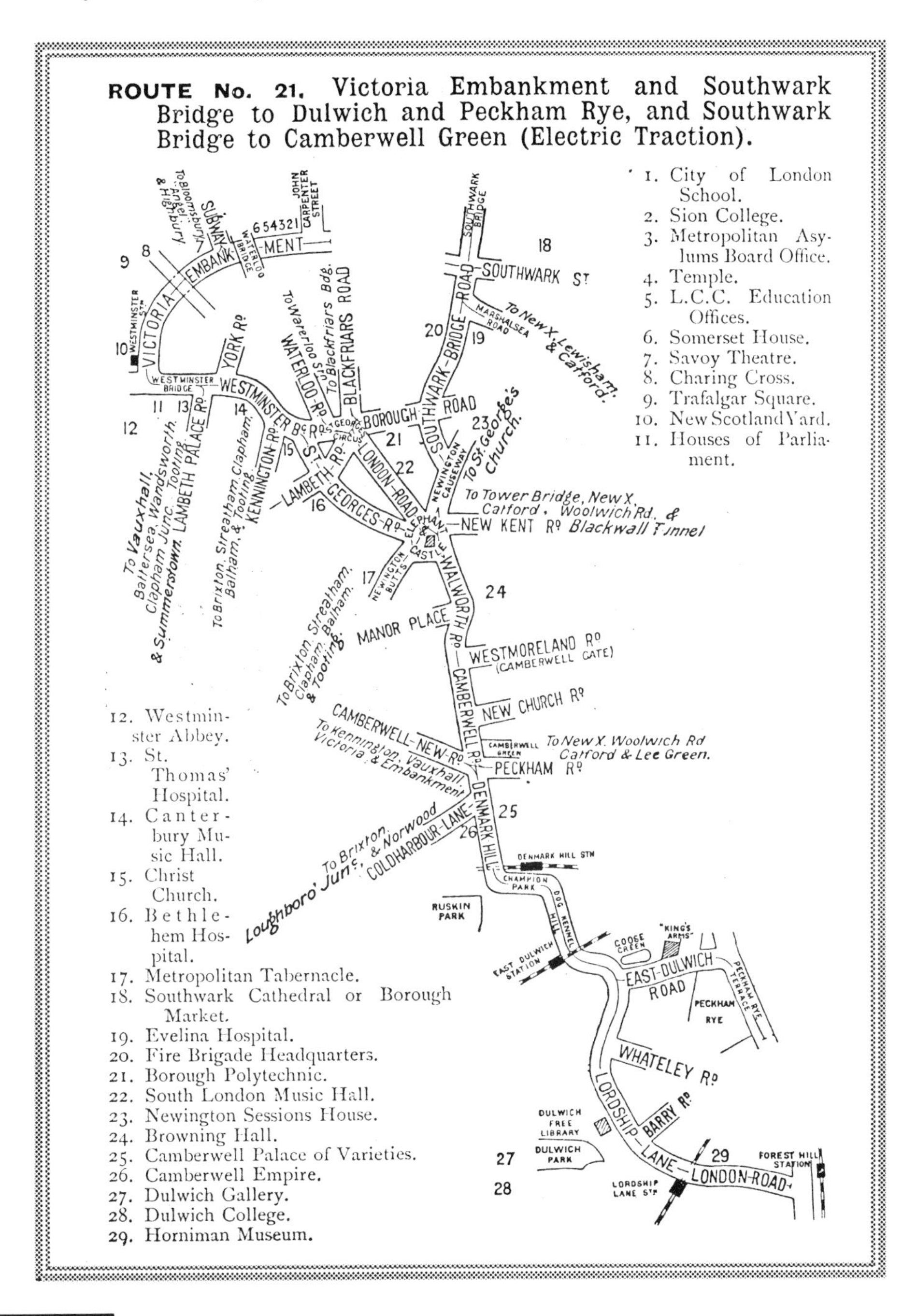

24. The railway bridge of East Dulwich Station extolls the virtues of a visit to the Co-op as car 1877 rounds the bend in Grove Vale. (C.Carter)

25. A glimpse across the roof tops from East Dulwich Station. An animated scene has been frozen by the camera, and if you look closely, the young lady running for the tram seems to be waving the temporary stop in her left hand! (National Tramway Museum)

26. Grove Vale leads to Goose Green and car 143 is about to turn left into East Dulwich Road. (John H.Meredith)

27. In September 1925, four wheel car 1696 bounces round the corner; this tram belonged to LCC class M and this group is fully described in *Greenwich and Dartford Tramways* in this series. (R.J.Harley Coll.)

561
PECKHAM RYE
WALWORTH RD
BISTO
for all
MEAT DISHES
143

PECKHAM RYE
DYES
1696

28. Summer comes to Goose Green. Maybe the driver of car 119 is reluctant to leave the leafy suburb for the more work-a- day world of the Victoria Embankment. Anyway, he pauses to pick up passengers whilst RT 1157 on route 37 waits at the bus stop. Those with broader

transport interests might like to know that this bus was delivered in April 1949 and worked from Nunhead (AH) Garage, which closed in 1954. (John H.Meredith)

2. Peckham Rye Branch

←

29. Not long before the fateful day a tram loads at a temporary "dolly" stop. These were rolled out after the fixed tram stops were removed. On the night of abandonment they were gathered up by LT officials and the new replacing bus stops were unveiled.
(Lens of Sutton)

31. An atmospheric view which could be titled "After the shower." Water vapour swirls around as sunlight catches the results of a recent downpour. A car on service 56 approaches the crossroads seen in the previous view. (R.J.S.Wiseman)

←

30. Bomb damage from the recent conflict is evident, as car 1877 crosses the junction East Dulwich Road with Peckham Rye. Note the tracks in the background curving round the edge of the Common towards the terminus. (John H.Meredith)

32. Chestnut paling fencing rings Peckham Rye Common, with the tram tracks close to the kerb and a sleepy noonday sun shining on the bright red and cream tramcar. (C.Carter)

56

56
EMBANKMENT
119

33. The LCC flats show up clearly through the late spring foliage as car 1878 nears the terminus. The driver of the lorry behind will not have to worry about which side of the road to overtake the tram for much longer, in a few months the tramway will have gone for good. (D.A.Thompson)

35. Shortly before the formation of London Transport in 1933, Richard Elliott snapped car 1892 resplendent in the last LCC livery of crimson and cream. (R.Elliott)

34. Car 119 waits for car 126 to leave the single track terminus at Peckham Rye. (John H.Meredith)

36. A final view of Peckham Rye terminus. One wonders how many local residents in these modern times would appreciate a return to the quality of service offered by the trams in 1951. (C.Carter)

B 6442

B LONDON TRANSPT T & T

The L.T. Exec. are not responsible for the loss of any luggage or damage thereto.

UP — This ticket must be retained by the passenger and handed to the Motorman in exchange for the luggage on completion of journey. — DOWN

AVAILABLE ON ONE TRAM ONLY

LUGGAGE

See over for further conditions.

Conditions on the reverse read - "personal or other luggage of a bulky nature or exceeding 28lbs in weight is to be carried on the front platform, and a charge of 2d per package made therefor. Luggage of a nature likely to impede the motorman or to be otherwise objectionable will not be carried. Issued subject to the bylaws and regulations of the LT Exec. To be shown on demand."
(B.Boddy coll.)

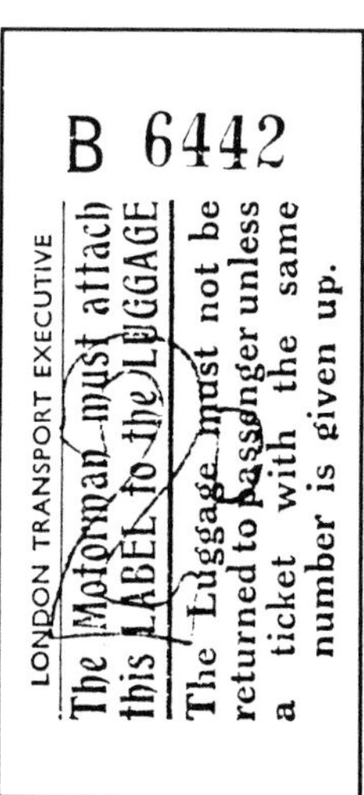

B 6442

LONDON TRANSPORT EXECUTIVE

The Motorman must attach this LABEL to the LUGGAGE

The Luggage must not be returned to passenger unless a ticket with the same number is given up.

3. Lordship Lane to Horniman Museum

37. We return to Goose Green to follow the fortunes of the other tram services travelling south. Note the horse trough in this view and the granite setted road surface which many cyclists and motorists will remember as rather treacherous when wet! (R.J.Harley Coll.)

62
FOREST HILL
BISTO
For all
MEATDISHES
TEA

58
BLACKWALL TNL
Launderette
213
PELLATT ROAD
1874

38. Accelerating away from the horse trough a service 62 tram rumbles along Lordship Lane on its way to Forest Hill. (John H.Meredith)

39. It would be unfair to say that the police sergeant on his bike constituted the rapid response squad at that time! In this evocative 1951 view, a Canterbury registered motor car is about to pass the tram which is taking on board a group of schoolgirls. Notice all the young ladies in this scene are wearing pristine white ankle socks which is perhaps a tribute to the effectiveness of the launderette and the Persil advert on the wall by Pellatt Road. (R.J.Harley Coll.)

40. Not a tower block in sight as we look along Lordship Lane towards Townley Road. Rehousing was tackled by the erection of prefabs, as seen to the right of the tram; each prefab had a small garden for the occupant. A far cry from the concrete jungles of the late 1950s and 60s which have caused more problems than they solved. (D.A.Thompson)

41. Opposite Barry Road, car 150 slows for the crossover at Dulwich Library. Behind the tram is the forecourt of *The Plough* public house which was used as a bus stand for routes 12 and 78. The high minded LCC had a policy of never naming a terminal after an adjacent public house. The London General Omnibus Company were less fussy, perhaps reflecting the "coaching inn" connections. LT tried to rationalise the situation and on many bus maps the forecourt terminal was referred to as *Dulwich Library*. However, when the trams went the boozy bus department reverted to type and the name *Dulwich Plough* was reinstated! (John H.Meredith)

ROUTE 58 | **Blackwall Tunnel - Forest Hill - Camberwell - Victoria** | **P.M. times are in heavy figures**

Via Tunnel Avenue, Blackwall Lane, Trafalgar Road, Romney Road, Nelson Road, London Street, South Street, Lewisham Road, High Street Lewisham, Rushey Green, Catford Road, Stanstead Road, Park Road, Waldram Road, Devonshire Road, London Road, Lordship Lane, Grove Vale, Dog Kennel Hill, Grove Lane, Champion Park, Denmark Hill, Camberwell New Road, Harleyford Road, Vauxhall Bridge, Vauxhall Bridge Road

RAILWAY STNS. SERVED : Greenwich, Lewisham, Catford Bridge, Catford, Forest Hill, Lordship Lane, East Dulwich, Denmark Hill, Oval, Vauxhall, Victoria.

Service interval : MONDAY to FRIDAY 6 mins. (peak hours 4 mins.), SAT. 4 mins. (early morn & eve. 5 mins.), SUN. morn 6 mins., afternoon 5 mins.

WEEKDAYS	First						Last		
BLACKWALL TUNNEL	....	....	....	....	....	5 40	10 20	11 20	....
Greenwich *Church*	..	..	..	..	5 22	5 48	X10 29	X11 29	..
Lewisham *Clock Tower*	....	....	....	....	5 30	5 56	X10 37	X11 37	12 3
Catford *Rushey Green*	..	..	..	5 22	5 39	6 5	X10 46	X11 46	12 12
Forest Hill *Station*	....	....	5 7	5 31	5 48	6 14	X10 55	X11 55	12 21
Lordship Lane *Goose Green*	4 20	§	5 19	5 43	6 0	6 26	X11 7	X12 7	12 33
Camberwell Green	4 30	4 39	5 29	5 53	6 10	6 36	X11 17	X12 17	12 43
VICTORIA *Clock Tower*	†4 52	4 55	5 45	6 9	6 26	6 52	X11 33	..	..
				§					
VICTORIA *Clock Tower*	§	....	†4 53	5 6	5 53	..	10 5	11 5	11 35
Camberwell Green	4 9	4 39	5 15	5 22	6 9	....	10 21	11 21	11 51
Lordship Lane *Goose Green*	4 19	4 49	5 25	5 32	6 19	..	10 31	11 31	12 1
Forest Hill *Station*	....	5 1	5 37	5 44	6 31	....	10 43	11 43	12 13
Catford *Rushey Green*	..	5 10	5 46	5 53	6 40	..	10 52	11 52	..
Lewisham *Clock Tower*	....	5 19	5 55	6 2	6 49	....	11 1	12 1	....
Greenwich *Church*	..	5 27	6 3	6 10	6 57	..	11 9	..	..
BLACKWALL TUNNEL	....	5 35	6 11	6 18	7 5	....	X11 18	....	....

SUNDAY	First				§					Last
BLACKWALL TUNNEL	....	....	....	....	7 40	C8 28	8 46	10 20	11 20	....
Greenwich *Church*	..	..	..	7 32	7 49	8 32	8 55	10 29	11 29	..
Lewisham *Clock Tower*	....	....	....	7 41	7 58	8 41	9 4	10 38	11 38	12 2
Catford *Rushey Green*	..	..	6 47	7 49	8 6	8 49	9 12	10 46	11 46	12 10
Forest Hill *Station*	§	....	6 55	7 57	8 14	8 57	9 20	10 54	11 54	12 18
Lordship Lane *Goose Green*	5 45	6 32	7 7	8 9	8 26	9 9	9 32	11 6	12 6	12 30
Camberwell Green	5 55	6 42	7 16	8 18	8 35	9 18	9 41	11 15	12 15	12 39
VICTORIA *Clock Tower*	6 10	6 55	7 29	B8 31	8 48	9 31	9 54	11 29	..	..
VICTORIA *Clock Tower*	..	6 14	6 59	..	7 33	..	..	10 4	11 4	11 34
Camberwell Green	6 16	6 29	7 14	7 36	7 46	....	....	10 18	11 18	11 48
Lordship Lane *Goose Green*	6 26	6 39	7 24	7 46	7 56	..	..	10 28	11 28	11 58
Forest Hill *Station*	6 37	....	7 35	7 57	8 7	....	....	10 39	11 39	12 9
Catford *Rushey Green*	6 45	..	7 43	8 5	8 15	..	..	10 47	11 47	..
Lewisham *Clock Tower*	....	....	7 51	8 13	8 23	....	....	10 55	11 55	....
Greenwich *Church*	..	..	8 0	8 22	8 32	..	..	11 4	..	..
BLACKWALL TUNNEL	....	....	....	C8 26	8 41	....	....	11 13	....	....

B–Time at St. Georges Church.
C–Time at Blackwall Lane.
X–1 minute earlier on Saturday.
†–Single journey to and from Charing X.
§–Early journey.

ROUTE 60	Dulwich - Camberwell - Elephant & Castle - City *Southwark*	P.M. times are in heavy figures

Via Lordship Lane, Grove Vale, Dog Kennel Hill, Grove Lane, Champion Park, Denmark Hill, Camberwell Road, Walworth Road, Newington Causeway, Borough High Street, Marshalsea Road, Southwark Bridge Road, Southwark Bridge

RAILWAY STATIONS SERVED : East Dulwich, Denmark Hill, Elephant & Castle, Borough

Service interval : MONDAY to FRIDAY peak hours 8 minutes ; SATURDAY morning peak hours 10 minutes, mid-day peak hours 8 minutes.

	MONDAY to FRIDAY												SATURDAY								
	Morning						Afternoon						Morning				Mid-day				
	First			Last			First			Last			First		Last		First			Last	
DULWICH *Library*	6 40	..	..	8 54	..	..	..	4 42	..	6 12	7 24	..	6 35	..	8 56	..	..	12 27	..	1 39	2 51
Lordship Lane *Goose Green*	6 44	....	....	8 58	....	..	....	4 47	....	6 17	7 29	....	6 39	....	9 0	....	....	12 32	....	1 44	2 56
Camberwell Green	6 54	..	..	9 8	..	..	3 43	4 57	..	6 27	7 39	..	6 49	..	9 10	..	11 30	12 42	..	1 54	3 6
Elephant and Castle	7 4	....	....	9 18	....	....	3 53	5 7	....	6 37	....	....	6 59	....	9 20	....	11 40	12 52	....	2 4	....
CITY *Southwark*	7 13	..	..	9 27	..	..	4 2	5 16	..	6 46	..	..	7 8	..	9 29	..	11 49	1 1	..	2 13	..
CITY *Southwark*	..	7 15	..	8 18	9 30	.	4 4	..	..	6 48	..	..	..	7 10	8 20	9 31	11 51	..	..	2 15	..
Elephant and Castle	....	7 24	....	8 27	9 39	....	4 13	....	....	6 57	....	....	....	7 19	8 29	9 40	12 0	....	....	2 24	....
Camberwell Green	6 24	7 34	..	8 37	9 49	..	4 23	..	..	7 7	..	..	6 19	7 29	8 39	9 50	12 10	..	..	2 34	..
Lordship Lane *Goose Green*	6 34	7 44	....	8 47	....	....	4 33	....	....	7 17	....	....	6 29	7 39	8 49	....	12 20	....	....	2 44	....
DULWICH *Library*	6 38	7 48	..	8 51	..	..	4 38	..	..	7 22	..	..	6 33	7 43	8 53	..	12 25	..	..	2 49	..

42. A smart gent with a briefcase hurries past the camera as the conductor of the terminating tram on the crossover practises the latest dance step. (John H.Meredith)

43. The breeze has got up, flapping the shop awnings and causing several ladies to hang onto their hats. The motorman of car 1866 is insulated from all this as he halts his charge on the Dulwich Common crossover in Lordship Lane. (John H.Meredith)

44. Another scene taken on Christmas Day 1950. This time Richard Wiseman has caught car 159 as it passes Horniman Gardens. Here we say good-bye to service 58; further coverage will be given in a later Middleton Press volume on Lewisham and Catford. (R.J.S.Wiseman)

4. Camberwell Green to Queen's Road

45. Back to Camberwell Green on the last day of 1950 and a seasonal scene finds a tram outbound to Woolwich battling against the elements. (R.J.S.Wiseman)

46. In brighter days east of the Green, we find car 1618 demonstrating one of the drawbacks of tram travel as the increase in motor traffic and LTs reluctance to install loading islands began to contribute to a rise in the accident rate. One alighting passenger looks nervously for approaching traffic, hoping that he will reach the kerb in one piece. (R.J.S.Wiseman)

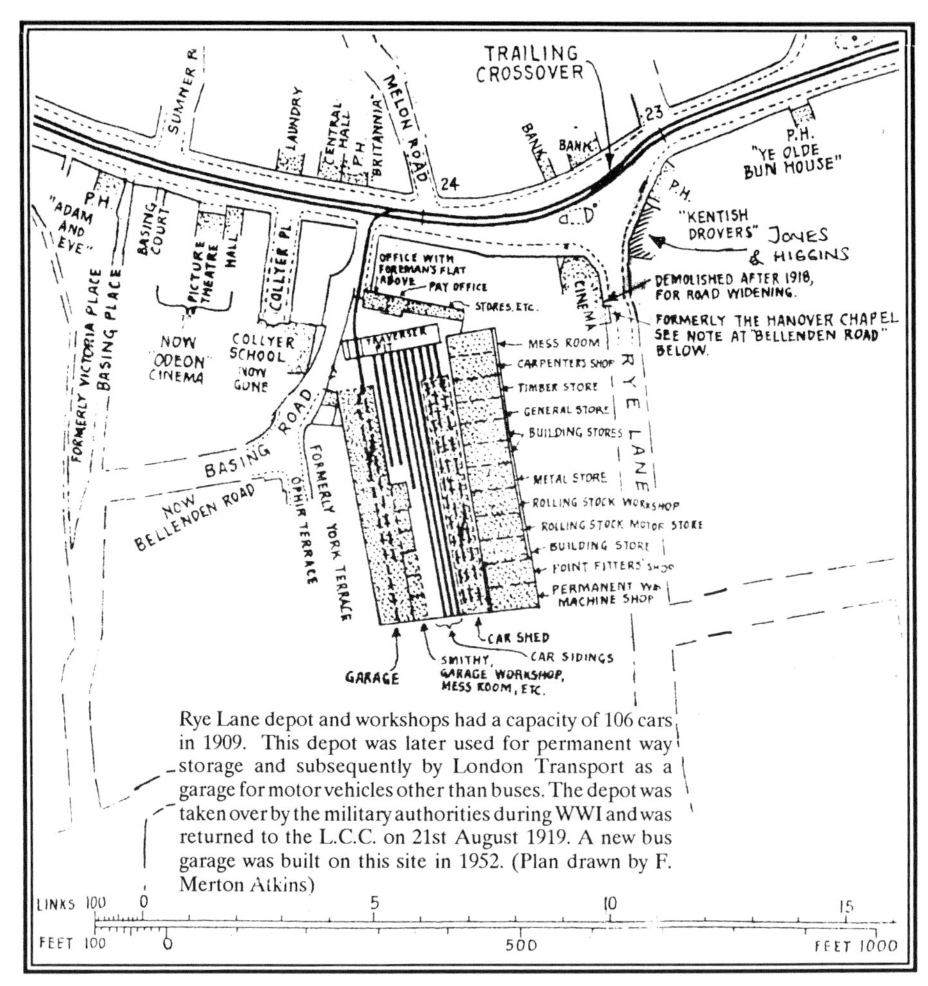

Rye Lane depot and workshops had a capacity of 106 cars in 1909. This depot was later used for permanent way storage and subsequently by London Transport as a garage for motor vehicles other than buses. The depot was taken over by the military authorities during WWI and was returned to the L.C.C. on 21st August 1919. A new bus garage was built on this site in 1952. (Plan drawn by F. Merton Atkins)

47. Peckham Rye Depot had a rather fitful existence in the electric era and it can best be described as an LCC outhouse where materials were stored, cars assembled and road vehicles were garaged. Just above LCC water car 02 at the edge of the depot canopy can be spotted the the two overhead wires which supplied power to a troller device whereby cars could be shunted around the depot. (D.Jones Coll.)

48. Jones and Higgins Corner, a well known Peckham landmark supplies the background for this early scene as LCC cars 277 and 342 make their sedate way to Waterloo Station and Westminster respectively. (C.Carter)

49. Where Peckham High Street joins Queen's Road at what was then Harders Road, a reversing stub was installed in 1914. By the time of this photo in June 1952 it was disused. Note the wonderful array of period vehicles as we look in a westerly direction past the *Red Cow* pub on the corner of Consort Road. (R.J.S.Wiseman)

40
PECKHAM METHODIST CHURCH
A SUNDAY WELL SPENT.
BRINGS A WEEK OF CONTENT.

51. Few people seem to be interested in car 196 as it passes under Queen's Road railway bridge in the last week of operation, July 1952. The motorman looks wistfully at the camera, perhaps he is reflecting that from next week when he takes out one of the replacing diesel buses, he will finally get to sit down as he travels the streets of South London! (R.J.S.Wiseman)

←

50. Looking east this time, a car on service 40 passes the Methodist Chapel which proclaims "A Sunday Well Spent Brings A Week Of Content." Unfortunately locals can no longer perform their devotions at this spot as the whole area has been sacrificed to the motor car, so that drivers can rush from one traffic jam to the next! (R.J.S.Wiseman)

52. A final view of Queen's Road is in the sunshine as the driver of car 1406 waits for the conductor's bell to signify the departure from the compulsory tram stop. The circle on these stops was blue in contrast to the red of the LT bus stop. (C.Carter)

ROUTE **78** | **West Norwood - Brixton - Vauxhall - Victoria** | **P.M. times are in heavy figures**

Via Norwood Road, Dulwich Road, Brixton Water Lane (return via Morval Road and Dalberg Road), Effra Road, Brixton Road, Stockwell Road, South Lambeth Road, Vauxhall Bridge, Vauxhall Bridge Road

RAILWAY STATIONS SERVED: West Norwood, Tulse Hill, Herne Hill, Brixton, Stockwell, Vauxhall, Victoria

Service interval: MON. to FRI. 6-8 mins. (eve. 10 mins.), SAT. morn. 8 mins., aft. and eve. 6 mins.

WEEKDAYS	First	Last
WEST NORWOOD *Thurlow Arms*	5 27	**11 3**
Herne Hill *Dulwich Road*	5 34	**11 10**
Brixton Road *Stockwell Road*	5 43	**11 19**
Stockwell *Swan*	5 47	**11 22**
Vauxhall *Station*	5 52	**11 27**
VICTORIA *Clock Tower*	5 59	**11 34**

	MON.-FRI. First	SAT. First		WEEKDAYS Last		
VICTORIA *Clock Tower*	6 2	6 3	....	**11 36**	..	....
Vauxhall *Station*	6 9	6 10	..	**11 43**	..	..
Stockwell *Swan*	6 14	6 15	....	**11 48**	..	....
Brixton Road *Stockwell Road*	6 18	6 19	..	**11 51**	....	..
Herne Hill *Dulwich Road*	6 27	6 28	....	12 0	....	....
WEST NORWOOD *Thurlow Arms*	6 34	6 35	..	12 7	..	..

5. Coldharbour Lane to Gresham Road

53. The change pit at the Camberwell end of Coldharbour Lane. The conductor stows the trolley pole as a service 34 car to Blackfriars prepares to leave, drawing power from the conduit. Note the plough shift attendant with his fork, ready to "plough up" the next northbound tram. (National Tramway Museum. H.B.Priestly)

54. Car 1996 arrives heading towards West Norwood. It has already "shot" its plough and it will now travel under the overhead to the terminus. (R.J.S.Wiseman)

55. Harry Williams in his book "South London" published as one of the "County" series in 1949, describes Coldharbour Lane as "a dismal thoroughfare." Whilst it isn't Mayfair, the honest toilers pictured here have the edge over the rich layabouts from the West End! True Londoners know you make the best of what you get. (R.J.Harley Coll.)

57. Fish and Chips, Watneys Ales and David Grieg encircle a 34 tram as it leads an RTL type bus past the end of Belinda Road.
(R.J.Harley Coll.)

←

56. In 1936 G.N.Southerden set up his camera at the junction with Herne Hill Road to record the white topped summer cap of the motorman leaning out from his service 34 car. He is waiting for the service 48 tram to clear the track as it approaches the points to swing to the right of the picture past the cyclist.
(G.N.Southerden)

58. Car 1384 finally quits Coldharbour Lane as it turns into Gresham Road.
(John H.Meredith)

59. At the end of Gresham Road was yet another change pit. This view was taken on 30th September 1950, in a few hours tramway activity at this location would cease for ever.
(R.J.S.Wiseman)

60. John Meredith was also present on the last day, but after it had started raining. Perhaps indulging in some valedictory ritual, the "who can put his trolley on the wire first" contest is in full swing! The replacing buses will be positively boring by comparison. (John H.Meredith)

LCC ticket, colour - light green and on the reverse side is an advertisement for Upson's Boots.

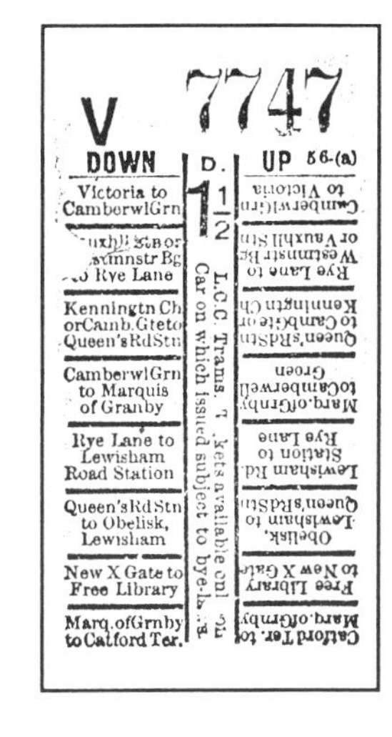

61. Looking down Gresham Road, the attendant is forking in the plough under car 192 as the driver causes the tram to edge slowly forward. (R.J.Harley Coll.)

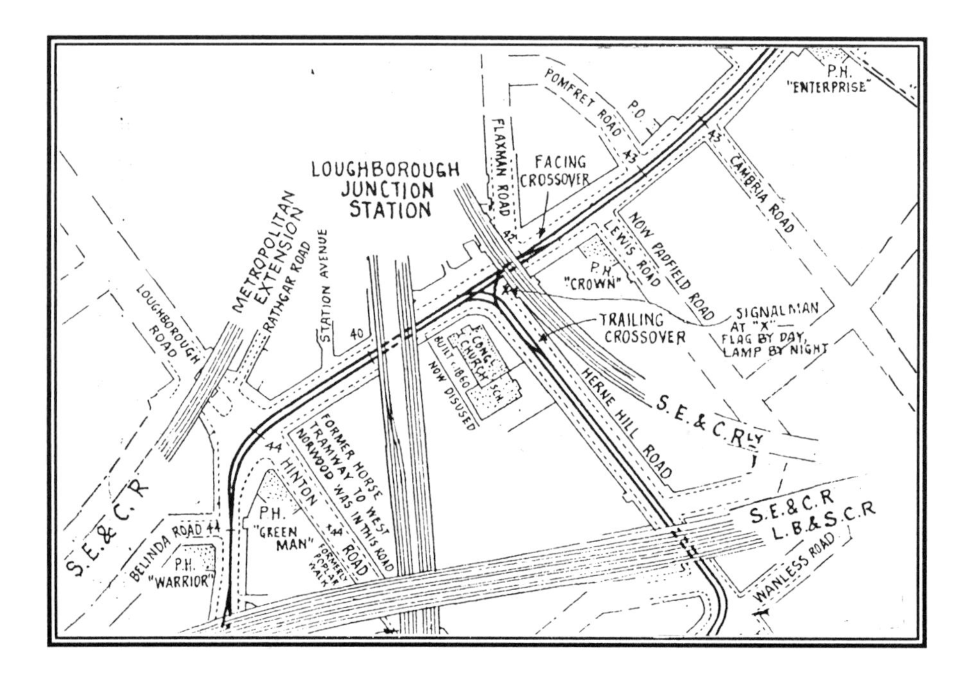

6. Loughborough Junction to West Norwood

62. Back at Loughborough Junction in the summer of 1951 a service 48 tram crosses into Coldharbour Lane. One hopes the coach seen through the lower saloon windows did not have to brake suddenly. (John H.Meredith)

63. Approaching the same bend as in the previous photograph, the motorman of car 1997 checks all is well before pulling out. Note the remains of former tracks which joined the western part of Coldharbour Lane and were last used in wartime diversions in 1941. (John H.Meredith)

March 1913

78 NORWOOD—VICTORIA STATION.
via Norwood Road, Dulwich Road, Effra Road, Stockwell Road, South Lambeth Road, and Vauxhall Bridge.
THROUGH FARE 3d.

	From		First Car	Last Car
Weekdays	From Norwood	..	First Car 5.21 am	Last Car 11.33 pm
	Victoria	..	6.0	12.10 am
Sundays	Norwood	..	8.36	11.29 pm
	Victoria	..	9.9	12.6 am

80 *NORWOOD—WATERLOO BDG. (Victoria Emb.)
via Norwood Road, Milkwood Road, Coldharbour Lane, Camberwell Green, Walworth Road, 'Elephant,' and Westminster Bridge.
THROUGH FARE 3d.

	From	First Car	Last Car
Weekdays	From Norwood	First Car 5.10 am	Last Car 8.15 pm
	Waterloo Bridge	5.59	9.0
Sundays to Camberwell Green only	Norwood	9.10	12.3 am
	Camberwell Grn.	9.31	12.32

64. The signal lamp on the standard next to the tram was taken from the Wimbledon route and used here at Loughborough Junction so that two trams did not meet on the single track. Before this, a controller was stationed here with a lamp at night and a flag during the day. (John H.Meredith)

65. Many people today (1993) don't know the difference between a tram and a trolleybus. However, there is not much excuse for the LT official who fastened this stop sign in Wanless Road. Perhaps he was inspired by the pre-war conversion scheme which would indeed have seen double the overhead and trolleybuses on route 648. More likely explanations are sloppiness or a wartime shortage of the correct tram stop signs. (C.Carter)

74 BRIXTON RD.—ST. GEORGE'S CHURCH.
via Coldharbour Lane, Camberwell Green, Walworth Rd., 'Elephant.'
THROUGH FARE 2d.

Weekdays	From Brixton Road	..First Car 5.57 am	Last Car 11.14 pm
	St. George's Ch..	6.24	11.10
Sundays	Brixton Road ..	8.30	11.20
	St. George's Ch..	8.57	11.17

†76* HERNE HILL—NEW BRIDGE ST., Blackfr's
via Effra Road, Brixton Rd., Kennington Park Road, 'Elephant,' and Blackfriars Bridge.
THROUGH FARE 2d.

Weekdays	From Herne Hill	..First Car 7.1 am	Last Car 8.8 p.m.
	New Bridge St..	7.37	8.45

This Service does not run on Sundays.

March 1913

CHEMIST
MEGGEZONES
Robins
48

48
MIST
GEZONES

66. A quiet, sunny day in December 1951 and a citybound 48 passes a group of small suburban shops in Milkwood Road as a southbound car waits to traverse the single track. It will then proceed down the righthand fork in the picture leading to Poplar Walk Road. (John H.Meredith)

67. This is the same junction as the previous view, but this time looking south. (R.J.S.Wiseman)

68. The corner of Poplar Walk Road and Lowden Road was a favourite for tramway enthusiasts and postbox fans. (J.H.Price)

69. The up and down tracks came together again further along Milkwood Road. This early LCC view taken before the First World War, shows car 1081 heading towards town on the Somerset House to West Norwood service. (D.Jones Coll.)

→

70. In the spring of 1948 car 1392 emerges from Lowden Road. Notice the motorcycle sidecar combination parked at the kerbside with a tarpaulin to keep off the rain. (John H.Meredith)

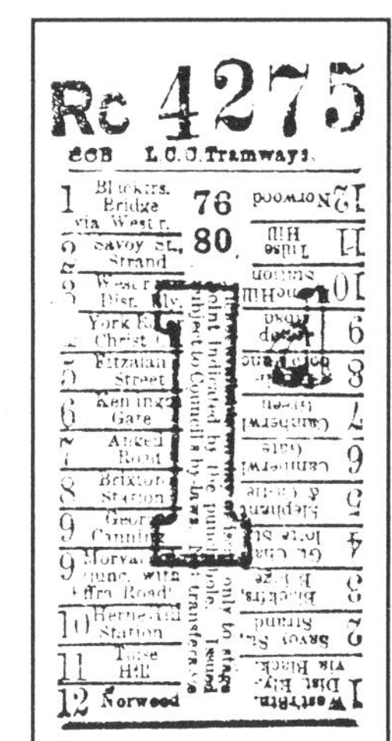

Rc 4275
L.C.C. Tramways.
76
80
1 Blckfrs. Bridge via West r.
2 Savoy St., Strand
Fitzalan Street
Gate
Brixton Station
10 Station
11 Tulse Hill
12 Norwood

ROUTE No. 23. Norwood to Victoria and Victoria Embankment (Waterloo Bridge), and Brixton Road to St. George's Church (Electric Traction).

1. Somerset House.
2. Savoy Theatre.
3. Charing Cross Stn.
4. Trafalgar Square.
5. New Scotland Yard.
6. Houses of Parliament.

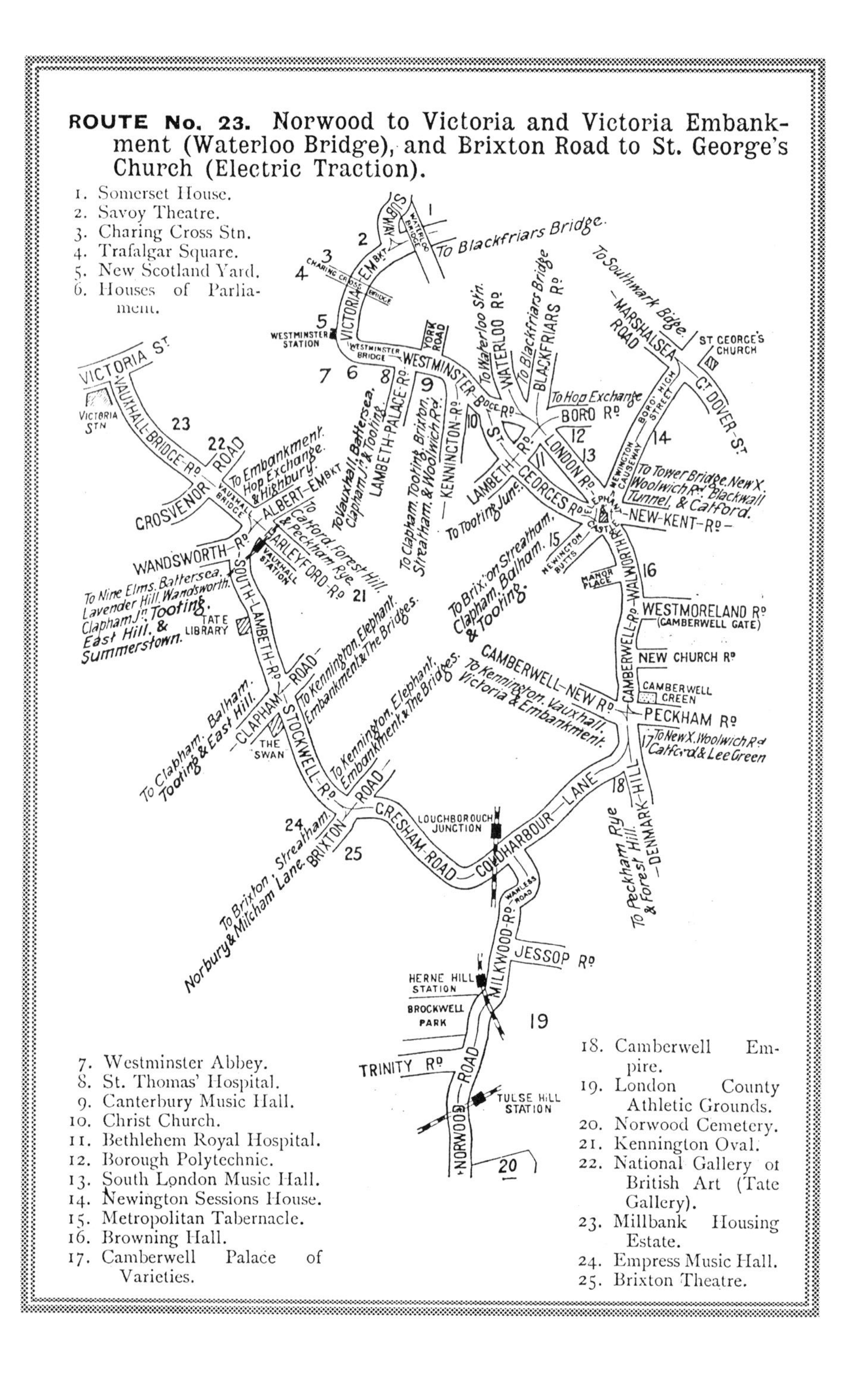

7. Westminster Abbey.
8. St. Thomas' Hospital.
9. Canterbury Music Hall.
10. Christ Church.
11. Bethlehem Royal Hospital.
12. Borough Polytechnic.
13. South London Music Hall.
14. Newington Sessions House.
15. Metropolitan Tabernacle.
16. Browning Hall.
17. Camberwell Palace of Varieties.
18. Camberwell Empire.
19. London County Athletic Grounds.
20. Norwood Cemetery.
21. Kennington Oval.
22. National Gallery of British Art (Tate Gallery).
23. Millbank Housing Estate.
24. Empress Music Hall.
25. Brixton Theatre.

71. Car 1941 rumbles over the crossover in Milkwood Road on a tranquil Sunday late in 1951. The route number stencil had been recut from an original service 18 version. That LT would go to such lengths to save money fairly reflects the opinions of the big-wigs at 55 Broadway towards the remaining tram routes. (John H.Meredith)

72. An ex-Leyton car 161 has swapped its East London environment for a leisurely run along a sunny Milkwood Road. Here the tramtracks parallel the railway from Loughborough Junction to Herne Hill, but neither tram seems in a hurry to race a competing electric train. (C.Carter)

73. The end is very near and the hooded bus stop is waiting to receive its first customers. Ironically the replacing 48 bus route was itself axed in August 1958 and Milkwood Road was finally deprived of public transport in December 1966. (R.J.S.Wiseman)

74. "Underneath the Arches" is a popular London song and its performance by Flanagan and Allen was calculated to bring tears to the eyes of many of those who lived in the "smoke." Many Londoners conducted business from premises similar to those by the queue waiting to board the tram. (R.J.S.Wiseman)

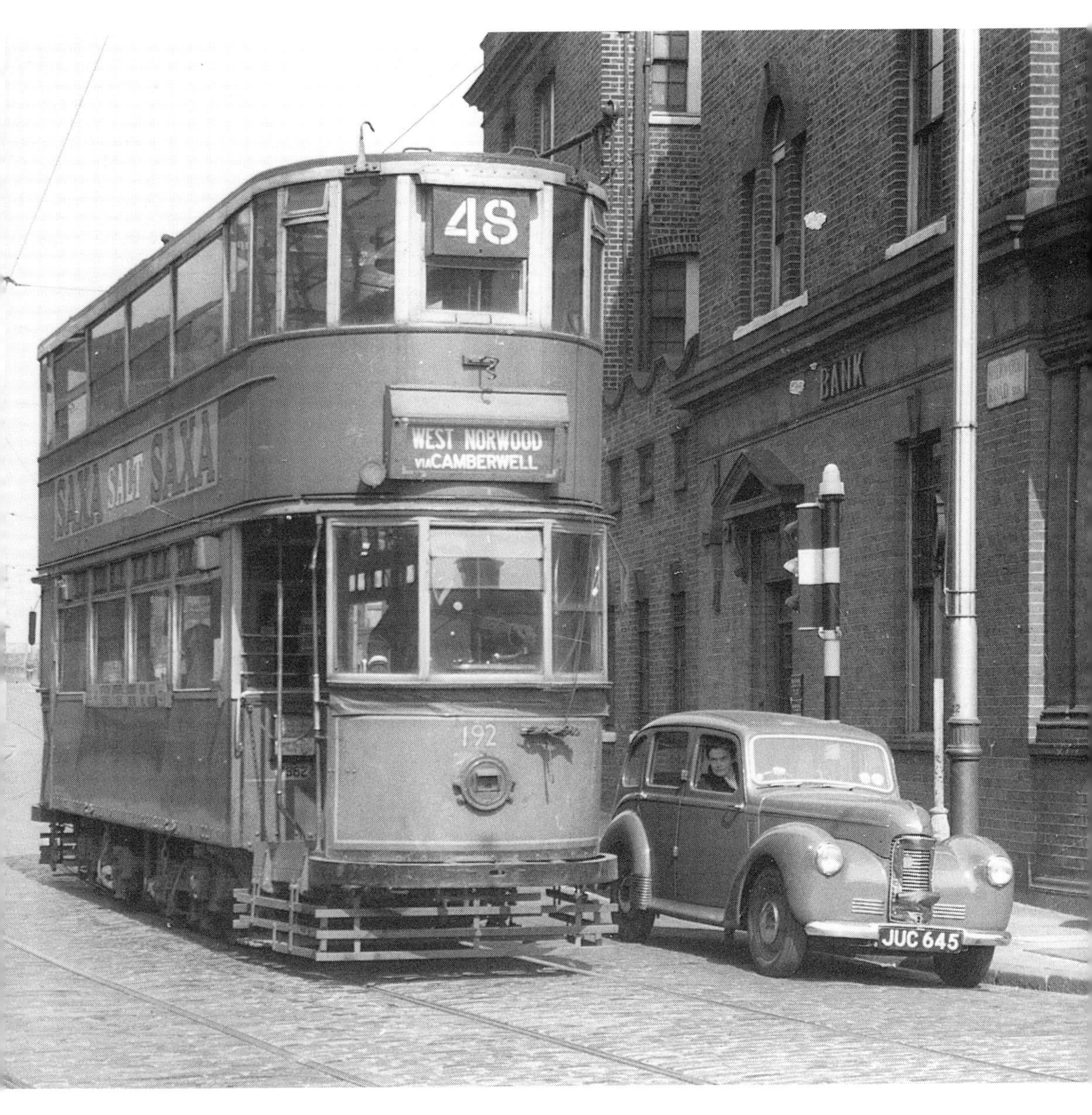

75. The motorman of car 192 waits for the lights before the sharp turn under Herne Hill railway bridge. (Lens of Sutton)

OUTHERN ELECTRIC — HERNE HILL
FREQUENT TRAINS TO WEST-END.
CITY & STATIONS TO ORPINGTON.
PRIVAT

48
CAMBERWELL
1991

48
CAMBERWELL
1387
ELECTRIC — HERNE HILL
TRAINS TO WEST-END
STEELE GRIFFITHS
KYP 917

76. The tram takes the spotlight as an RT bus scurries away in the shadows past the Tram Pinch sign warning motorists of an impending encounter with several tons of tramcar! (John H.Meredith)

lower left

77. Into Norwood Road by Brockwell Park service 48 was joined by the 33 and 78. Underneath the blue and white RAC direction sign is the hooded points indicator for tramdrivers - left for Brixton and straight on for Camberwell. Readers interested in railways might like to note that a similar view taken after the trams ceased, is included in the Middleton Press album *Victoria to Bromley South*. (John H.Meredith)

78. The northbound track behind car 1941 was laid close to the kerb by Brockwell Park, hence another Tram Pinch warning sign to the left of the tram. This particular tram was one of two cars, 1938 was the other, used as late Saturday staff cars which ran Norwood, Oval, Camberwell Green, Milkwood Road and back to Norwood Depot. Both trams were designated "quiet" cars! (John H.Meredith)

33
and Hovis and butter for tea
Esso
1940

78
VICTORIA
BRIXTON
RED BARREL
PHONE. RODNEY 2188
Ashfords
LAUNDRY LTD.
CAMBERWELL
IRVINE
LTD
GIP 5092
TUL 5756
193

79. The single track opposite Trinity Rise is safely negotiated by car 1940. Prominent on this tram is the "Via Kingsway Subway" indicator above the main blind; service 33 used this underground connection in the centre of London to reach its northern destination of Manor House. (John H.Meredith)

81. The clip-clop of tram horses is heard outside the Tulse Hill Hotel. Car 29 is extolling the virtues of the Daily Express at a halfpenny a copy; the horse bus heading in the opposite direction invites people to invest in a box of Bryant and Mays matches. (J.H.Price Coll.)

80. Service 78 terminated at Victoria and car 193 squeezes between a builder's lorry and a laundry van just before the single track. (Lens of Sutton)

82. Over half a century after the previous photo, the clock reads just before midday as car 183 basks in the December sunshine of a 1951 day. (John H.Meredith)

83. Perran Road crossover, Tulse Hill and a bright day in 1950 sees a service 48 car nearing its terminus. Note the pads in the road for activating the traffic lights at the road junction. (John H.Meredith)

84. New brickwork on the abutments to Tulse Hill railway bridge betray the wartime repairs after a flying bomb struck the area on 29th July 1944. Picture 22 in the Middleton Press book *Mitcham Junction Lines* gives a better idea of the devastation. Happily the tram seen here is in more peaceful times as it picks up passengers on a gloomy November day in 1951. (R.J.S.Wiseman)

85. The railway bridge is in the background as we pause outside Norwood Depot. A crew member walks past buses which had been parked at the tram depot as an overflow measure due to the nearby bus garage receiving extra vehicles for the Festival of Britain special services in 1951. (R.J.S.Wiseman)

86. The entrance to Norwood Depot reflects municipal pride in a classical LCC tramway style. Notice the wooden seat thoughfully placed for those elderly and infirm enthusiasts who just wanted to watch the trams sway by. (John H.Meredith)

87. Further along the approach track, we meet car 02 again, now in LT red livery. The open platform looks very inviting for an illicit tram driving session! (John H.Meredith)

88. Inside, most of the fifteen depot roads are empty; the capacity was originally 61 bogie cars, but towards the end only 46 trams were stabled there. On 5th April 1952 with the closure of service 33, the depot said good-bye to its trams and the building, which still survives, was eventually sold by LT. At least it never suffered the indignity of becoming a bus garage. (John H.Meredith)

89. A solid row of late Victorian buildings welcomes us as we observe LCC car 1532 on service 80 which was inaugurated in 1909 and lasted until November 1933, when service 48 was extended to cover part of the route. (R.J.Harley Coll.)

90. A pony and trap saunters along the tramlines in this pre-1914 view. From the look of it, the conductor of car 1010 seems to be keeping a wary eye on the trolley rope. (J.H.Price Coll.)

91. This postcard was sent in February 1907 and the horse car in the picture was under threat of electrocution. (J.H.Price Coll.)

92. Almost at the end of our journey and car 1921 waits to enter the terminal stub at West Norwood. On the pavement is a section feed box with a departmental telephone to contact HQ. This was used by LT employees and the number was listed in the official timetable as OT 159.
(National Tramway Museum. H.B.Priestley)

93. Car 1948 having received the right of way to enter the terminus, leaves sister car 1940 in front of the *Thurlow Arms*.
(National Tramway Museum./R.B.Parr)

33
MANOR HOUSE
VIA WESTR & ESSEX RD
1948
and butter is better

WILLIAMSON
WEST NORWOOD
1088
CANNON
BREWERY

WILLIAM
E. VINCENT
& SONS
GENERAL
BUILDERS
MERCHANTS
76
2A
GENERAL

94. Back at the *Thurlow Arms* again, but this scene belongs very much to the beginning of the twentieth century. All the activity suggests a thriving community with the trams an essential part of daily life. (R.J.Harley Coll.)

95. Time has moved on in this view and already the motor bus is becoming a serious competitor. Note that the tramlines now extend across the road junction to a terminus adjacent to St. Luke's Church. (R.J.Harley Coll.)

96. The date is 22nd March 1952 and the days of tramways at West Norwood are numbered. Car 179 seems to be suffering from amnesia and doesn't quite now where it is going; hopefully the driver will soon attend to the front indicator blind. (John H.Meredith)

97. A fine broadside view of LCC car 1546 at West Norwood terminus. The year is 1928 and service 76 has but three more years to run before it is replaced by service 33. (R.J.Harley Coll.)

ROUTE **48** — West Norwood - Camberwell - Elephant & Castle - City *Southwark* — P.M. times are in heavy figures

Via Norwood Road, Milkwood Road (return via Poplar Walk Road and Lowden Road), Hinton Road, Coldharbour Lane, Denmark Hill, Camberwell Road, Walworth Road, Newington Causeway, Borough High Street, Marshalsea Road, Southwark Bridge Road, Southwark Bridge

RAILWAY STATIONS SERVED: West Norwood, Tulse Hill, Herne Hill, Loughborough Junction, Elephant and Castle, Borough

Service interval: WEEKDAYS 10 mins. (peak hours 8 mins.), SUNDAY 10 mins.

	WEEKDAYS First		MON. to FRI. Last				SAT. Last			SUNDAY First		SUNDAY Last	
	*												
WEST NORWOOD *Thurlow Arms*	5 6	5 23	10 52	11 22	....	....	1 28	11 2	11 23	8 8	....	11 10	11 22
Herne Hill *Station*	5 13	5 30	10 59	11 29	..	..	1 35	11 9	11 30	8 15	..	11 17	11 29
Camberwell *Green*	5 24	5 41	11 11	11 41	....	....	1 46	11 20	11 41	8 26	....	11 28	11 40
Elephant & Castle	..	5 51	11 21	..	..	..	1 56	T11 34	..	T8 38	..	T11 40	.
CITY *Southwark*	....	6 0	11 30	....	....	....	2 5	....	....	....	....	....	..
CITY *Southwark*	*	6 2	11 32	....	....	....	2 7	....	....	....	....	....	....
Elephant & Castle	..	6 11	11 41	..	..	..	2 16	T11 38	..	T8 40	..	T11 42	..
Camberwell *Green*	5 26	6 21	11 51	....	....	....	2 26	11 52	....	8 52	....	11 54	....
Herne Hill *Station*	5 37	6 32	12 3	..	..	..	2 37	12 3	..	9 3	..	12 5	..
WEST NORWOOD *Thurlow Arms*	5 44	6 39	12 10	....	....	....	2 44	12 10	....	9 10	....	12 12	....

*-Special early journey. T-Time at St. Georges Church.

SPECIAL EARLY JOURNEYS-SUNDAY

Norwood to Victoria, via Herne Hill, Stockwell, Vauxhall Bridge at 6 24, 7 15 a.m.
Norwood to Waterloo Bridge, via Herne Hill, Brixton, Kennington Road and Westminster Bridge at 6 54 a.m.
Norwood to Stockwell at 7 32 a.m.
Victoria to Norwood, via Vauxhall Bridge, Stockwell, Herne Hill at 7 0, 7 50 a.m.
Waterloo Bridge to Norwood, via Westminster Bridge, Kennington Road, Brixton, Herne Hill at 7 33 a.m.
Stockwell to Norwood at 7 52 a.m.

7. Herne Hill to Effra Road

98. We return to Herne Hill Station to follow the direct route to Brixton latterly traversed by services 33 and 78. However, this view dates before the introduction of service numbers in 1912, and we see car 1101 on its journey to Victoria. Transport for the better off is provided by the two taxis on the rank outside Brockwell Park. (J.H.Price Coll.)

99. A final look at the elevated railway signal box at Herne Hill which looks over this 1952 scene. Services 48 and 78 have already perished and the overhead under the bridge has been dismantled. Soon service 33 will be no more and the buses and private cars will have the roadway to themselves. (John H.Meredith)

33
KINGSWAY SUBWAY
WEST NORWOOD
...and Hovis and butter for tea
1988
AUL 169

ENSINGS
HOVIS
HOVIS
33
WEST NORWOOD
TEA
NO ENTRY
1946

100. The side roads off Dulwich Road evoke some of the greats of English literature. Here a tram passes over the crossover opposite Chaucer Road; it will shortly encounter Spencer Road, Shakespeare Road and Milton Road. The obituaries had already been written for the London tramcar and the songs of praise emanating from LT would chorus a Brave New World of flexible bus services. (John H.Meredith)

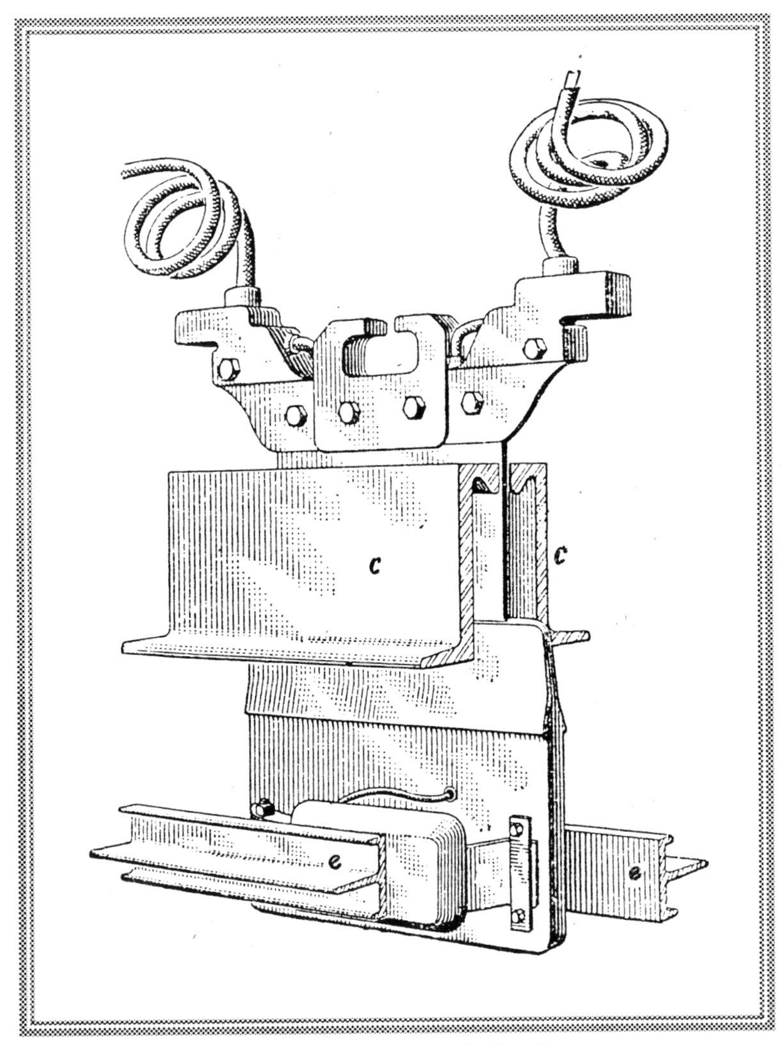

Original Long Lead Plough.
c = slot rail e = conductor rail

101. Car 1946 has just emerged from Dalberg Road whilst the citybound track curves left into Brixton Water Lane. (John H.Meredith)

102. In retrospect it is easy to say that the flats being constructed to the right of the tram in Dalberg Road were the beginning of the downward path in British architecture. The terraced houses in the rest of the road represent a more traditional social order. (R.J.Harley Coll.)

103. A last view of Dalberg Road before the war-damaged Taylor Walkers pub was pulled down to make way for the flats.
(John H.Meredith)

33
MANOR HOUSE
WESTR & ESSEX RD
...and Hovis and butter for tea
FISH & CHIPS
NO ENTRY
2000
DPL 508

33
STOP
2000

104. The fleet number of the tram turning past the "George Canning" into Effra Road, reminds us of the coming millenium and the hope of many that modern trams will return to the streets of London. (John H.Meredith)

106. "The road goes on forever"...well not quite, but the rails and wires lead to a vanishing point at the Brixton end of Effra Road. (C.Carter)

105. No, we haven't got the picture the wrong way round! Reversed service number stencils were an LT oddity which the strict LCC would never have tolerated. The scene is the foot of Effra Road with the track into Morval Road curving towards the left. (John H.Meredith)

ROUTE **33** | **West Norwood - Westminster - Islington - Manor House** | P.M. times are in heavy figures

Via Norwood Road, Dulwich Road, Brixton Water Lane (return via Morval Road and Dalberg Road), Effra Road, Brixton Road, Kennington Park Road, Kennington Road, Westminster Bridge, Victoria Embankment, Kingsway Subway, Theobalds Rd., Rosebery Avenue, Upper Street, Essex Rd., Dove Rd. (return via Balls Pond Rd.), Mildmay Park, Green Lanes

RAILWAY STATIONS SERVED: West Norwood, Tulse Hill, Herne Hill, Brixton, Oval, Lambeth North, near Waterloo, Westminster, Charing Cross, near Aldwych, Holborn, Angel, Essex Road, Manor House

Service interval: MON. to FRI. 8 mins. (peak hours 6 mins.); SAT. 6 mins. (before 9 0 a.m. 7½ mins.); SUN. morn. 12 mins., aft. and eve. 8-10 mins.

	MONDAY to FRIDAY First		Last			SATURDAY First	Last				SUNDAY First	Last		
WEST NORWOOD *Thurlow Arms*	4 58	....	10 6	10 48	....	4 58	9 54	....	10 48	....	8 15	9 52	....	10 48
Herne Hill *Dulwich Road*	5 5	..	10 13	10 55	..	5 5	10 1	..	10 55	..	8 22	9 59	..	10 55
Kennington Gate	5 19	....	10 28	11 10	....	5 20	10 16	T10 35	11 10	....	8 36	10 13	T10 34	11 9
Waterloo Bridge *Embankment*	5 33	..	10 42	11 24	..	5 34	10 30	10 39	11 24	..	8 48	10 25	10 38	11 21
Bloomsbury *Southampton Row*	5 37	....	10 46	11 28	....	5 38	10 34	10 43	11 28	....	8 52	10 29	10 42	11 25
Islington *Angel*	5 45	..	10 55	..	..	5 46	10 42	10 52	11 37	.	9 0	10 37	10 50	..
St. Pauls Road *Canonbury*	5 53	....	11 3	....	....	5 54	10 51	11 0	....	....	9 7	10 44	10 57	....
MANOR HOUSE *LT Station*	6 4	..	11 14	..	..	6 5	11 1	11 10	..	..	9 18	10 55	11 8	.
MANOR HOUSE *LT Station*	5 12	....	11 16	....	....	5 12	11 10	11 12	....	....	8 23	11 0	....	11 12
St. Pauls Road *Canonbury*	5 23	..	11 27	..	..	5 23	11 20	11 22	..	..	8 34	11 11	..	11 23
Islington *Angel*	5 31	....	11 35	..	....	5 31	11 2[illegible]	11 31	....	....	8 41	11 19	....	11 31
Bloomsbury *Southampton Row*	5 39	..	11 44	..	..	5 39	11 37	..	..	..	8 49	11 26	11 28	..
Waterloo Bridge *Embankment*	5 43	....	11 48	....	....	5 43	11 41	....	....	....	8 53	11 30	11 32	....
Kennington Gate	5 57	..	12 2	..	..	5 57	11 55	..	..	..	9 5	11 42	11 44	....
Herne Hill *Dulwich Road*	6 11	....	12 17	....	....	6 12	12 10	....	....	....	9 19	11 56	11 58	..
WEST NORWOOD *Thurlow Arms*	6 18	..	12 24	..	..	6 19	12 17	..	..	..	9 26	12 3	12 5	..

FOR ADDITIONAL JOURNEYS SEE ROUTE 48

EARLY MORNING JOURNEYS — Norwood *Depot* to Savoy Street, SUNDAY at 6 38 a.m.
Bloomsbury to Highgate, SUNDAY at 5 0 a.m.
Bloomsbury to Manor House, MON. to FRI. at 4 40, 5 27 a.m.; SAT. at 4 41, 5 27 a.m., SUNDAY at 6 0, 7 0, 8 0 a.m.
Islington *Angel* to Manor House, MON. to FRI. at 3 51, 4 34, 5 0, 5 12 a.m.; SAT. at 3 51, 4 34, 5 6 a.m.; SUNDAY at 8 2, 8 26, 8 38, 8 50 a.m.
Islington *Sub Station* to Manor House, MON. to FRI. at 5 24 a.m.; SAT. at 5 23 a.m.
Manor House to Bloomsbury, WEEKDAYS at 4 12, 4 58 a.m.; SUNDAY at 6 31, 7 31 a.m
Highgate to Bloomsbury, SUNDAY at 5 31 a.m.
Highgate *LT Garage* to Bloomsbury, SUNDAY at 4 31 a.m.
Highgate *LT Garage* to Islington *Sub Station*, MON. to FRI. at 5 7 a.m.; SAT. at 5 5 a.m.
Highgate *LT Garage* to Islington *Angel*, MON. to FRI. at 3 32, 4 15, 4 41, 4 53 a.m.; SAT. at 3 31, 4 14, 4 46 a.m.; SUNDAY at 7 43, 8 7, 8 19, 8 31 a.m.
Savoy Street to Norwood *Depot*, SUNDAY at 7 13 a.m.

LATE NIGHT JOURNEYS—Westminster *LT Station* to Highgate, MON. to FRI. at 10 40 p.m., 12 0 midnight; SUNDAY at 10 56, 11 7, 11 26 p.m.
Westminster *LT Station* to Highgate *LT Garage*, SUNDAY at 11 14 p.m.
Islington *Angel* to Highgate *LT Garage*, SAT. at 11 10, 11 16, 11 31, 11 33, 11 37 p.m.
Highgate to Westminster *LT Station*, MON. to FRI. at 11 23 p.m.
Highgate to Highgate *LT Garage*, SUNDAY at 11 31, 11 42 p.m., 12 1 a.m.

T–Time at Westminster *Station*.

107. At the junction of Brixton Hill and Effra Road, car 177 edges forward drawing power from the overhead; in a few seconds the plough will be ejected from the tram. (R.J.S.Wiseman)

108. The plough carrier was fixed between the two bogies and here a plough is guided under its own momentum towards the centre storage road. Three spare ploughs wait to be forked under cars bound for inner London. (John H.Meredith)

109. "A streetcar named EX" doesn't trip off the tongue very easily. In fact, this two letter code denoted an extra car, inserted as and when required by passenger loadings or route changes. Note the patriotic display by the owner of Orange Luxury Coaches. (John H.Meredith)

110. There was little need for pedestrian, traffic free zones when this photo was taken, and the fact that anyone could wander about in the middle of the main road to town in almost complete safety was an accepted part of life. (R.J.Harley Coll.)

ROLLING STOCK

Every London book in the Tramway Classics series will concentrate on several main car types which operated on the capital's tramways. In this volume we will look at LCC car 1 and classes HR2 and E3.

LCC car 1 was constructed by the council as a prototype for a new fleet of trams; needless to say the arrival of LT in 1933 put paid to this idea. The car first appeared in May 1932 and it was finished in a livery of royal blue and white; it was used on services 33 and 35. Later in the 1930s it was repainted in LT red and after the war it was sold to Leeds. Happily the car was rescued and it now resides at the National Tramway Museum in Crich, Derbyshire.

111. Seen at West Norwood in brand new condition, car 1 had a degree of style and sophistication unmatched by any bus. (G.N.Southerden)

112. The crew appointed to handle the council's "new baby" were hand picked, so it is no wonder that the motorman is gently coaxing the trolley towards the overhead. Piloting the flagship of the fleet was a prestigious job. (G.N.Southerden)

113. The top deck provided well upholstered seats for the travelling public. (D.Jones Coll.)

114. The seats in both saloons were covered in blue moquette, and were arranged in staggered pairs to ease passenger movement. Here we see inside the lower saloon. (D.Jones Coll.)

LCC no.1 was know as *Bluebird* on account of its first livery. All drawings are to the scale of 4mm to 1ft.

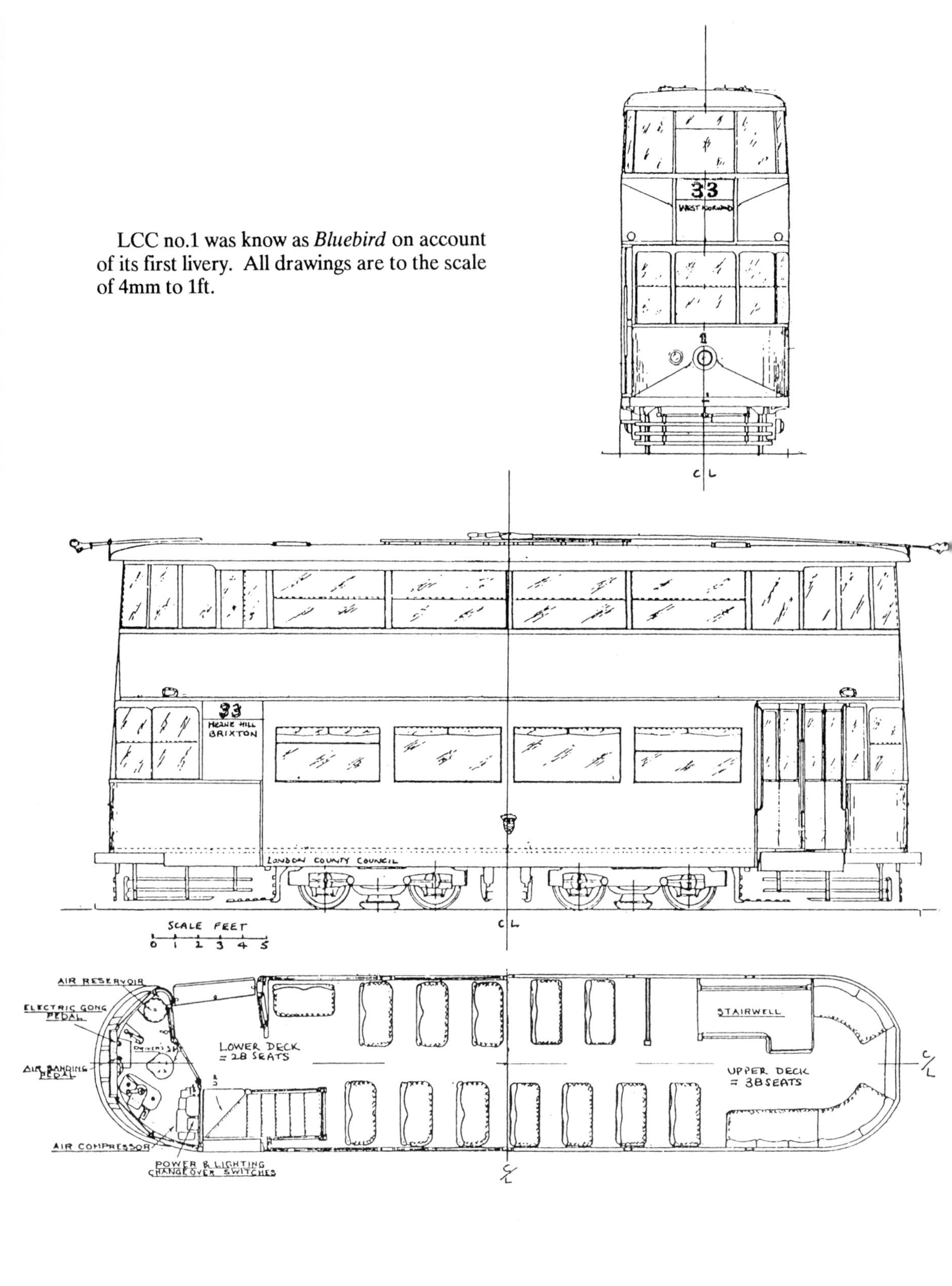

HR2

The HR2 type was developed as a work-horse for services operating over steep gradients. Therefore it was natural that they should feature on Dog Kennel Hill, where the four motor cars could show their prowess.

115. An experimental car was built as a test rig for the later HR2 type. This platform view is of car 1852 which was designated HR1; it was still not equipped with a windscreen, as the Metropolitan Police did not favour enclosed platforms. (R.J.Harley Coll.)

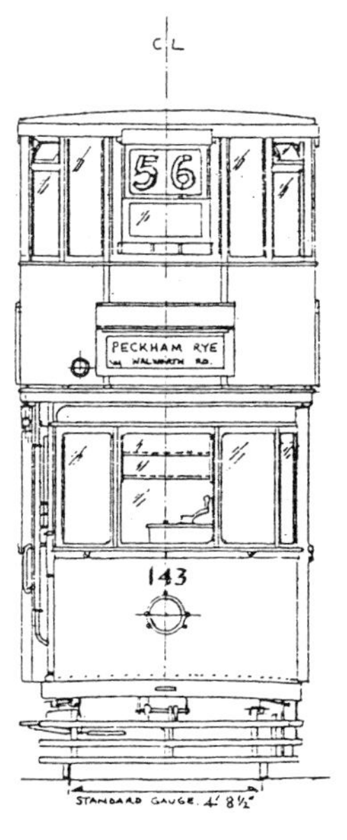

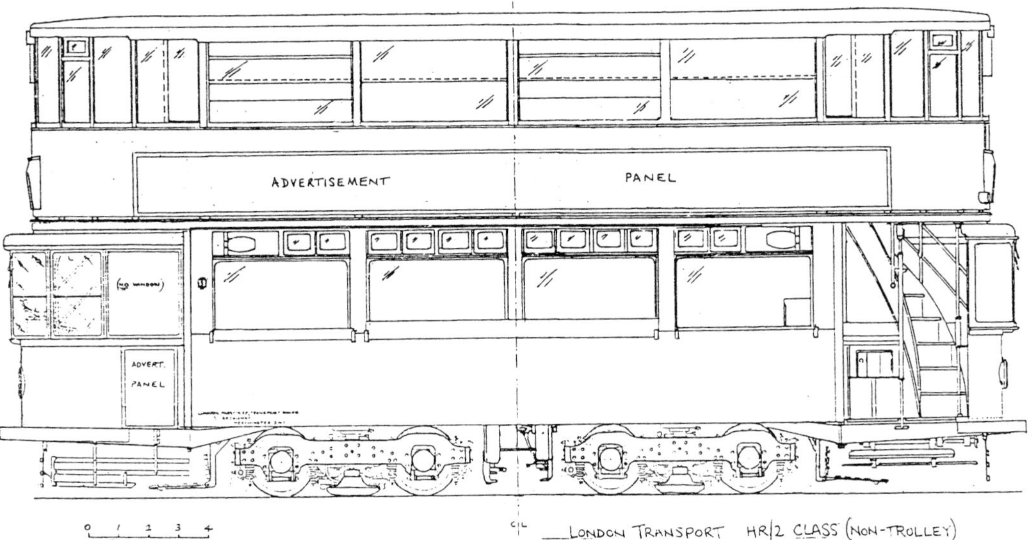

116. A fine photo of car 1883 newly delivered and working service 56 to Peckham Rye. (R.Elliott)

117. This view shows the clean lines of the all metal body giving a lower deck which was both functional and comfortable. (J.H.Price Coll.)

118. Some photographers have all the luck! John Meredith was standing on the corner of Champion Park when he caught all the possible permutations of HR2 cars in one view. Car 122 has a timber windscreen and no trolley poles; car 1893 was damaged in the war and rebuilt witha timber top deck. Car 1880 on service 60 is a standard car of the earlier batch, numbered 1854-1903, with trolley poles and non-radial arm trucks. The distant car on service 58 is from the later batch numbered 101-160, with no trolley poles, radial arm trucks and Alpax metal windscreens. Finally car 1890 on service 84 is a pre-war rehabilitated car with route number blind. (John H.Meredith)

119. Car 1862 is on an enthusiasts' special at West Norwood. (John H.Meredith)

E3

Class E3 cars were delivered primarily for working the new double deck Kingsway Subway services; they were numbered 1904-2003. The bodywork was identical to that supplied for the HR2 class. The trucks were the more traditional maximum traction style favoured by the LCC and a number of other tramway operators in London.

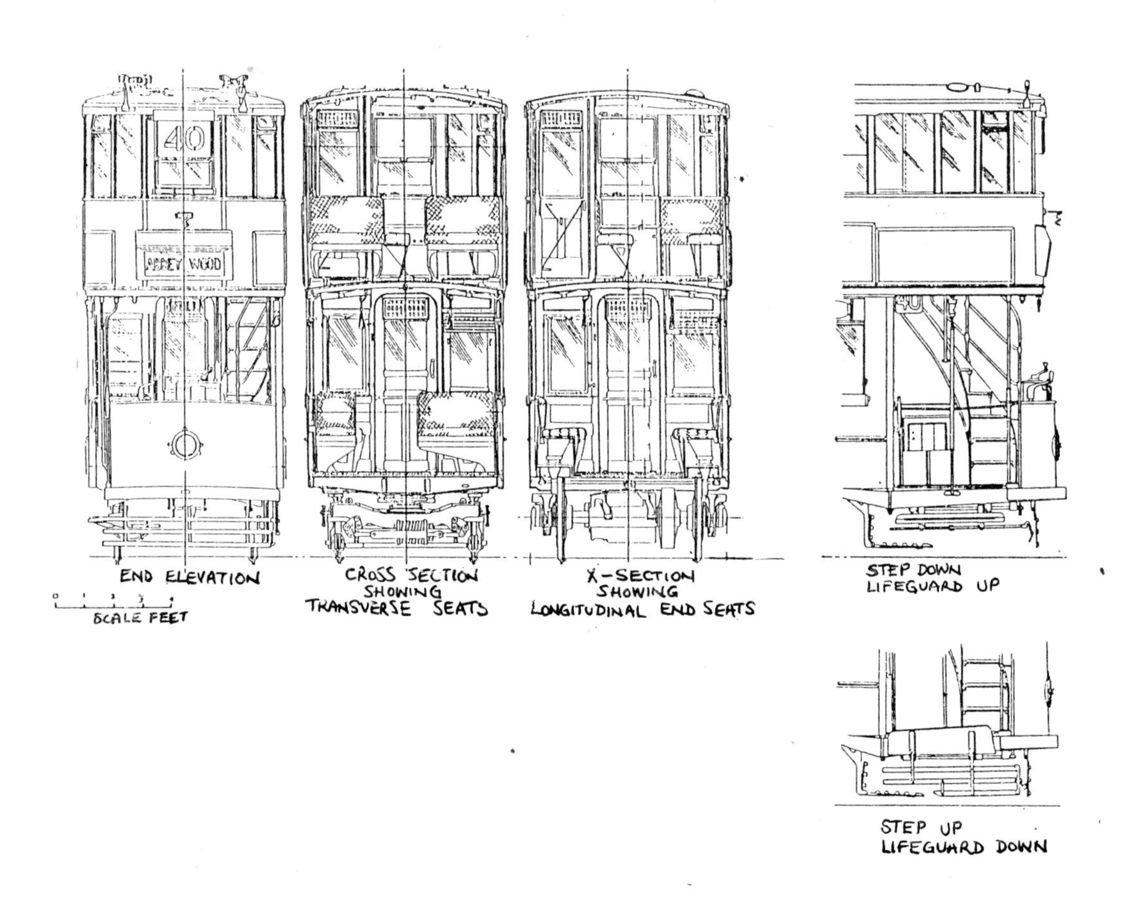

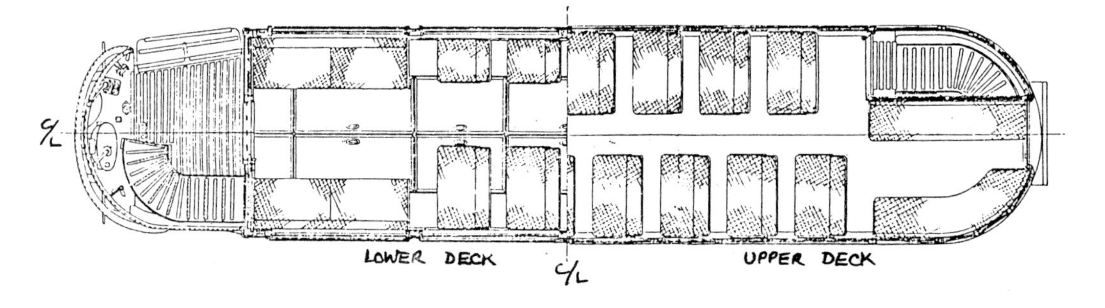

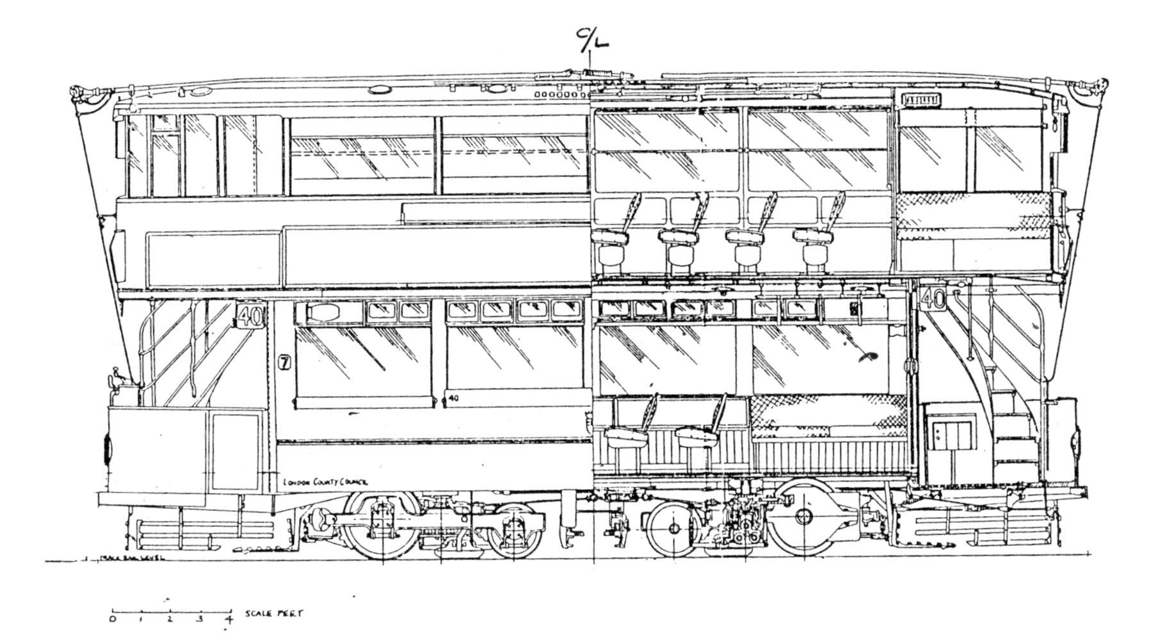

120. Richard Elliott snapped car 1905 at Abbey Wood in "as delivered" condition without an Alpax windscreen. It was advertising itself as "one of the 150 new and better trams for South London." (R.Elliott)